CHELS

Champions of E1
1954-55

DESERT ISLAND FOOTBALL HISTORIES

CLUB HISTORIES	ISBN
Aberdeen: A Centenary History 1903-2003	1-874287-57-0
Aberdeen: Champions of Scotland 1954-55	1-874287-65-1
Aberdeen: The European Era – A Complete Record	1-874287-11-2
Bristol City: The Modern Era – A Complete Record	1-874287-28-7
Bristol City: The Early Years 1894-1915	1-874287-74-0
Cambridge United: The League Era – A Complete Record	1-874287-32-5
Cambridge United: 101 Golden Greats	1-874287-58-9
The Story of the Celtic 1888-1938	1-874287-15-5
Chelsea: Champions of England 1954-55	1-874287-94-5
Colchester United: Graham to Whitton – A Complete Record	1-874287-27-9
Coventry City: The Elite Era – A Complete Record	1-874287-83-X
Coventry City: An Illustrated History	1-874287-59-7
Dundee: Champions of Scotland 1961-62	1-874287-86-4
Dundee United: Champions of Scotland 1982-83	1-874287-71-6
History of the Everton Football Club 1878-1928	1-874287-14-7
Halifax Town: From Ball to Lillis – A Complete Record	1-874287-26-0
Hereford United: The League Era – A Complete Record	1-874287-18-X
Hereford United: The Wilderness Years 1997-2004	1-874287-83-X
Huddersfield Town: Champions of England 1923-1926	1-874287-88-0
Ipswich Town: The Modern Era – A Complete Record	1-874287-43-0
Ipswich Town: Champions of England 1961-62	1-874287-63-5
Kilmarnock: Champions of Scotland 1964-65	1-874287-87-2
Luton Town: The Modern Era – A Complete Record	1-874287-90-2
Luton Town: An Illustrated History	1-874287-79-1
Manchester United's Golden Age 1903-1914: Dick Duckworth	1-874287-92-9
The Matt Busby Chronicles: Manchester United 1946-69	1-874287-96-1
Motherwell: Champions of Scotland 1931-32	1-874287-73-2
Norwich City: The Modern Era – A Complete Record	1-874287-67-8
Peterborough United: The Modern Era – A Complete Record	1-874287-33-3
Peterborough United: Who's Who?	1-874287-48-1
Plymouth Argyle: The Modern Era – A Complete Record	1-874287-54-6
Plymouth Argyle: 101 Golden Greats	1-874287-64-3
Plymouth Argyle: Snakes & Ladders – Promotions and Relegations	1-874287-82-1
Portsmouth: From Tindall to Ball – A Complete Record	1-874287-25-2
Portsmouth: Champions of England – 1948-49 & 1949-50	1-874287-50-3
The Story of the Rangers 1873-1923	1-874287-95-3
The Romance of the Wednesday 1867-1926	1-874287-17-1
Stoke City: The Modern Era – A Complete Record	1-874287-76-7
Stoke City: 101 Golden Greats	1-874287-55-4
Potters at War: Stoke City 1939-47	1-874287-78-3
Tottenham Hotspur: Champions of England 1950-51, 1960-61	1-874287-93-7
West Ham: From Greenwood to Redknapp	1-874287-19-8
West Ham: The Elite Era – A Complete Record	1-874287-31-7
Wimbledon: From Southern League to Premiership	1-874287-09-0
Wimbledon: From Wembley to Selhurst	1-874287-20-1
Wimbledon: The Premiership Years	1-874287-40-6
Wrexham: The European Era – A Complete Record	1-874287-52-X

WORLD CUP HISTORIES	
England's Quest for the World Cup – A Complete Record	1-874287-61-9
Scotland: The Quest for the World Cup – A Complete Record	1-897850-50-6
Ireland: The Quest for the World Cup – A Complete Record	1-897850-80-8

MISCELLANEOUS	
Red Dragons in Europe – A Complete Record	1-874287-01-5
The Book of Football: A History to 1905-06	1-874287-13-9
Football's War & Peace: The Tumultuous Season of 1946-47	1-874287-70-8

CHELSEA

Champions of England
1954-55

Series Editor: Clive Leatherdale

Rob Hadgraft

DESERT ISLAND BOOKS

First published in 2004
by
DESERT ISLAND BOOKS LIMITED
89 Park Street, Westcliff-on-Sea, Essex SS0 7PD
United Kingdom
www.desertislandbooks.com

© 2004 Rob Hadgraft

The right of Rob Hadgraft to be identified as author of this work has been
asserted under The Copyright Designs and Patents Act 1988

British Library Cataloguing-in-Publication Data
A catalogue record for this book is available from the British Library

ISBN 978-1-874287-94-0

Printed in Great Britain
by
4Edge Ltd

Contents

PAGE

Author's Note   6
Preface, by Derek Fowlds   7

INTRODUCTION: THE PENALTY-KICK THAT MADE HISTORY   8

1. FOUNDATIONS (1905-52)   17

2. DRAKE TAKES THE HELM (May 1952 – June 1954)   28

3. THE LULL BEFORE THE STORM (August-September 1954)   39

4. FALLING OFF THE PACE (October-November 1954)   50

5. THE MARVELS OF MUDDY MOLINEUX (December 1954)   60

6. MOUNTING A SERIOUS CHALLENGE (January-February 1955)   102

7. TO THE TOP OF THE PILE (March 1955)   114

8 THE GLORIOUS FINALE: NUTS IN THE BOARDROOM (April 1955)   124

9 HOW THE MIGHTY FELL (POST-1955)   136

Guide to Seasonal Summaries   147
Seasonal Summaries   148

AUTHOR'S NOTE

The week I was born, in 1955, reigning League champions Chelsea slumped into the nether regions of Division One. No doubt this fact escaped my attention at the time. All these years later, however, the footballing events of the mid-1950s have become a matter of great interest to me. I am pleased to have been commissioned to examine events leading up to, and beyond, the day when Chelsea became England's unlikely champions.

It was a fascinating period in the history of a fascinating football club, and deserving of a book as we head for the fiftieth anniversary of that momentous day. I am grateful to a number of people who assisted with research, including Tony Banks MP, Richard Posner, Alan Scoltock, Alec McKay, Les Dennis, Kieran Clifton, and Adrian Linden, not forgetting the staff of the Newspaper Library at Colindale. I can also personally recommend Roy Bentley's conducted tours around Stamford Bridge, which are organised by the football club's PR department. The stadium may be much-changed, but Chelsea's former skipper has a treasure trove of memories about the 1955 era, and you won't leave short-changed.

Select Bibliography: *Ninety Years of the Blues*, Ron Hocking (1995); *The Legends of Chelsea*, Scott Cheshire (2003); *Stamford Bridge Legends*, David Lane (2003); *Chelsea: Football Under the Blue Flag*, Brian Mears (2001); *Jimmy Greaves*, Matt Allen (2001); *Greavesie*, Jimmy Greaves (2004); *King John*, John Charles (2004); *Ron Reynolds: The Life of a 50s Journeyman Footballer*, Bowler/Reynolds (2003); *Sam Bartram by Himself* (1956); *Charles Buchan's Soccer Gift Book* (1955); *Autobiography*, Tom Finney (2004); *Clown Prince of Soccer*, Len Shackleton (1955); *Parliamentary Debates*, Hansard, HMSO; *Explaining English Character*, Geoffrey Gover; *John Major: The Autobiography* (2000); *The Grit in the Oyster*, Keith Proud (2003); *London in the Twentieth Century*, Jerry White (2002).

ROB HADGRAFT

PREFACE

I began watching Chelsea when I was twelve (in 1949-50) and I have joined forces to write this Preface with a dear friend of mine called Basil Weissand, who is now 81 years old and has been watching The Blues since he was five. So between us we have notched up quite a few hours at Stamford Bridge.

In this highly entertaining book, author Rob Hadgraft has certainly captured the wonder and the excitement of that magical year when Chelsea won the title. Let's hope our next championship is just around the corner.

This book will provide a great read for all true supporters of Drake's Ducklings. Manager Ted Drake was ably assisted by Dickie Foss, a great former Chelsea player who became Ted's right-hand man as he created the 1954-55 team.

The book means we can once again glory in the exploits of the heroes in blue who helped to win the First Division championship for the first and only time in our history. Great names like Roy Bentley, our captain and leading goalscorer for many years, Eric ('The Rabbit') Parsons, Frankie Blunstone, Peter Sillett, Ken Armstrong, Stan Willemse, the two amateur internationals Jim Lewis and Seamus O'Connell, and, of course, Ron Greenwood, who later became the England manager.

We used to sit high in the sky in the new North Stand in 1954-55 and were proud to be 'ever presents' during the greatest season in our club's history.

That North Stand has now gone, but I am sure the new generation of true-blue Chelsea supporters will have great success to look forward to. And as long as we have in our midst men like Gianfranco Zola, we need not fear the future.

DEREK FOWLDS*
Colerne, Wiltshire

* *Actor Derek Fowlds, 67, is best known for his TV roles as Bernard in* Yes Minister, *Oscar Blaketon in* Heartbeat, *and Mr Derek on* The Basil Brush Show. *Despite his success in showbusiness, Derek's feet are kept firmly on the ground by the ups and downs of Chelsea FC, and by his long-time girlfriend Jo, who says 'all actors are wallies'.*

THE PENALTY-KICK THAT MADE HISTORY

Easter Saturday, 9th April, 1955. Hazy late afternoon sunshine casts shadows over London SW6. On the Fulham Road, the scullery clocks tick slowly toward 4.30pm. Inside the packed Stamford Bridge football ground nearby, mayhem reigns. A colossal crowd of 75,000 cannot believe what they have just witnessed.

In a match locked in goalless stalemate after seventy-five minutes' play, young Chelsea forward Seamus O'Connell – an amateur who traded cattle during the week – had swooped on the ball, just inside the Wolves' penalty area, to unleash a powerful drive towards the top of the net. The shot eluded the clawing dive of keeper Bert Williams and arrowed unerringly towards the top left-hand corner of the goal. Suddenly, seemingly from nowhere, flaxen-haired Billy Wright, the thirty-one-year-old captain of England, leaped upwards to fist the ball over the bar. 'Penalty' roared the crowd, to a man, their wide-eyed screams amplified by the gut-wrenching anxiety of the previous seventy-four goalless minutes.

On the field, eleven sets of Chelsea arms shot to the sky in a collective appeal that was hardly necessary, so clear-cut had been the offence. All eyes fell on Leicester referee J W Malcolm. After what seemed an age, Mr Malcolm pointed dramatically to his right. He'd given a corner!

The players and crowd were momentarily stunned. The most blatant handball seen at Stamford Bridge in many moons had been missed by the referee. The chance to convert a penalty that would beat mighty Wolves and sew up the First Division championship was being denied. Chelsea's moment of unprecedented glory was thrown in doubt due to one man's inexplicable lapse of judgment.

When a 75,000-throng is provoked by a common grievance, the only possible outcome is mayhem. The sheer intensity of the rage directed at Mr Malcolm seemed likely to crush his light frame and flatten him to the Stamford Bridge turf. Within moments the official is engulfed by a mob of frantic Chelsea players. A couple of burly defenders, including fearsome Stan Willemse, raced half the length of the pitch to reach him, revealing a turn of speed rarely seen in their normal game. But this was an injustice of massive proportions and the Chelsea players were not about to let the hapless perpetrator off the hook.

The ugly kerfuffle and sheer volume of protests forced Mr Malcolm, whether willing or unwilling, over to the touchline. By now he presumably sensed in his bones that he has 'missed' something. Fortunately for Chelsea, the linesman did not shirk his responsibilities. In common with almost everyone else in the stadium, he had seen Billy Wright's handball. So penalty it was, after all.

Now the focus of attention switched from the sweating, pale figure of the referee. Chelsea full-back Peter Sillett, an ox of a defender, picked up the ball and placed it on the penalty-spot. Sillett, just twenty-one, but weighing fourteen stones and a powerful belter of a football, took responsibility for the most important kick of a ball in his club's history. The job couldn't have gone to a better man. Single-minded and reliable, Sillett oozed the determination needed for such a pressure situation. He had only recently taken over the job of penalty-taker, and had netted three out of three, following a miserable mid-season run that saw colleagues miss five spot-kicks in succession. Sillett surely wouldn't miss. He wouldn't even entertain the idea.

Sillett would later admit that, like the referee, he hadn't been sure what happened after O'Connell's shot sped goalwards, and accepted that he and Mr Malcolm must have been the only two people in the ground who failed to see the handball. Consequently he was not 'going potty' like the rest of the team. He recalled the forty-yard walk to the penalty spot, during which all sorts of comments were directed his way, some of it well-meaning advice, some of it clearly not. One sideways remark, from Wolves winger Johnny Hancocks, would stick in his mind: 'He'll stick it in the net.' Chelsea manager Ted Drake also recalled seeing Sillett throw a glance at him as the player strode forward. 'He read my mind,' said Drake, enigmatically.

As Sillett carefully placed the ball, the racket from the sun-drenched crowd subsided to a low hum. The tension was so great that some spectators could not bear to look. Up at the Shed End, grown men covered their faces and their knees knocked. If Sillett scored, the resistance of defending champions Wolves would surely crumble. Victory will then be Chelsea's and will carry them to within a point or two of their first title in this, their Golden Jubilee year. This is not just a penalty-kick at a football match: it's a life-defining moment for tens of thousands of people.

The entire episode will last less than three minutes, but will remain etched for ever in the memory of all who witness it. Later it will be revealed that among the thousands of wide-eyed youngsters in the crowd that day was future Prime Minister John Major and future Sports Minister Tony Banks, both of whom still eulogise about the occasion.

Sillett was an oasis of calm as players jostled for position on the eighteen-yard line. Although he possessed a famously fierce shot, he was not known as a blaster of penalties. He normally liked to place them into the corner, employing a disdainfully short run-up of barely two strides. Never did Chelsea need their King of Cool as much as now. His deceptive casualness was well-known at Stamford Bridge, and the fans wondered whether Sillett would maintain his poise in this tense atmosphere.

Although outwardly calm, Sillett betrayed his inner feelings by affording this penalty a bit more respect than usual. He purposefully stepped back from the ball by several more strides than normal. Thirty-five-year-old Wolves and England goalkeeper Bert Williams is as experienced as they come, but even he looked tense as Sillett shaped up. Thus far Williams had repelled everything that Chelsea have thrown at him, but now came the moment of truth. This game, the two points, and almost certainly the championship, rested on this moment.

The crowd strained to get the best possible view of Sillett, and some had already worked out what the extra steps meant. There were gasps as the penny dropped. He must be planning to blast this one, instead of sliding it into the corner. Up he came, clouting the ball with all the power he was famous for. The ball flew low and hard to Williams' right, billowing the net around two feet off the ground and a similar distance from the stanchion. Williams had no chance, even though he chose correctly which way to dive.

Stamford Bridge erupted and Sillett disappeared under a mob of excited teammates. Barring a stunning collapse, the championship was now in the bag. Unbelievable. Chelsea, the national joke team that never won anything – never even came close – were set to become Champions of England. Only something freakish could now spoil the party. Wolves exerted enormous pressure in remaining minutes, with Johnny Hancocks prominent, but the home side grimly hung on. Then, with a flourish and a whistle from Mr Malcolm, it was all over.

Chelsea (three games left) had gone seven points clear of Wolves (six games remaining). Although the title was not mathematically secure, all were agreed it was as good as won. Even having three games in hand would be of little help to out-of-form Wolves.

Sports-Minister-to-be Tony Banks celebrated his twelfth birthday the day before the Wolves game. He attended every Chelsea home match that season, but has no doubt that Sillett's penalty was the most memorable drama: 'That sticks out in my mind as the moment we really clinched the title. There was a huge crowd and I remember how they literally rolled the smaller lads like me over the heads of the adults in front so we could get down the front for a better view. We were passed out onto the greyhound track and watched the match from there, sitting on the straw that protected the track. Kids were often passed to the front like this and there was never a problem with it.'

And future Prime Minster John Major would later admit that seeing Sillett's penalty sink Wolves was the moment he found himself 'hooked for life' to the Chelsea cause. This was one of Major's first visits to see Chelsea. He too was only twelve (and like Tony Banks, his birthday came shortly before the game). Major had recently moved with his family to Coldharbour Lane in Brixton, some three miles from Stamford Bridge.

Another lad in the crowd that day was Richard Posner, who grew up to become a West End property consultant. He recalls: 'Peter Sillett marched up to blast the penalty home – how England could have done with his penalty-taking in later years! Everyone went mad when it went in, although as a seven-year-old I have to admit I didn't really understand the full significance of the day or the event.'

Chelsea winger Frank Blunstone later recalled Sillett's change of approach to this particular kick and marvelled at the way he'd 'smashed the ball with all his might' instead of slotting it in as normal. Blunstone felt the win that day proved Chelsea could defend and grind out results when necessary. He reckoned much of the massive tension of that day stemmed from a feud between the two managers – Ted Drake and Stan Cullis – who had what he described as a 'punch-up' on the touchline the previous season when Wolves beat the injury-hit Blues 8-1. Certain remarks by Cullis were said to have provoked Drake. Blunstone believed Drake wanted to beat Wolves as much as he wanted to win the title.

Chelsea goalkeeper Chick Thomson told one interviewer that the players coped well with the tension of that day, but their manager was not so relaxed. Drake apparently spent the night beforehand wandering around Wimbledon Common unable to sleep. He returned home in the early hours in a bedraggled state.

Chelsea fan Alec McKay, nowadays living in the USA, recalls that Wolves were the side to beat during that era: 'At the time, Wolves were the glamour team with those cool gold and black uniforms.' Chelsea historian and statistician Ron Hockings says that on top of the 75,000 packed inside the ground, there were many thousands straining for news outside. He believes Billy Wright would have been sent off for his hand-ball in modern times, but in those days a penalty was seen as sufficient punishment, even though in this case it very nearly wasn't awarded.

As the crowd slowly dispersed, some fans probably reflected on what a difference a day can make in football. Just twenty-four hours earlier, the club's title hopes had looked shaky, following a 1-1 Good Friday draw with Sheffield United at Stamford Bridge. Chelsea had looked tense and disjointed. Now, here they were, shaking off the fatigue of two games in two days, and beating the best side in the country, who themselves had spent the previous few days taking the sea air at Ramsgate.

Drake had somehow instilled in his troops the need to forget Sheffield United and focus on the coming ninety minutes with Wolves. The healthy 50,000 crowd which turned up for the Good Friday game was effectively doubled to see Wolves, with 75,043 squeezing inside and an estimated 25,000 locked out. The gates had closed forty-five minutes before kick-off with mounted police attempting to keep order and encouraging the unlucky late arrivals to go home. Most ignored those appeals and hung around to follow the progress of the game via the roars and groans from inside the ground. Ten minutes before the teams took to the field, thousands inside the ground had jumped the rails to squat on the greyhound track, with police and officials powerless to get them back.

Once the game was over and the stadium emptied, the fans next task was to find an updated League table. National newspapers had been halted by strike action for the past fortnight. In fact, the table showed not only that Wolves had a mountain to climb to catch Chelsea, but the other challengers (Portsmouth, Manchester City and Sunderland) also faced a near-impossible task. This was how the table read, for those who could find one to read:

	P	W	D	L	F	A	Pts
Chelsea	39	19	11	9	77	55	49
Manchester C	37	17	9	11	70	58	43
Wolves	36	16	10	10	79	58	42
Portsmouth	36	17	8	11	65	51	42
Sunderland	38	12	17	9	56	51	41

The papers hit the streets again just in time to cover Chelsea clinching the championship on St George's Day, Saturday 23rd, with an almost anticlimatic 3-0 win over hapless Sheffield Wednesday, who were already relegated and thereby short on competitive instincts. That game came nowhere near the excitement of Wolves; in fact the most memorable scenes against Wednesday took place after the final whistle.

Chelsea finished the season with 52 points, a tally that will remain the lowest ever, now that the modern game rewards three points for a win. Accusations that they were 'lucky' were perhaps inevitable, with detractors pointing to inconsistency by the likes of the more-fancied Wolves,

Portsmouth and Manchester United. 'Chelsea didn't win the title, Wolves threw it away', was a popular theme. Another accusation was that Drake's heroes had bullied their way to victory, employing crude tactics to stifle skilful opposition. Although it has to be agreed that Chelsea did adopt an uncompromising approach, they also fielded a number of players who relied on skill and brains rather than simply brawn.

Skipper Bentley was a classic example of a talented player who could also 'mix it' when required. Nowadays, Bentley guides visitors on tours of Stamford Bridge and happily takes questions about how the title was won. He tells how Drake drummed into them the need to be positive and attacking in outlook, and would expect the wingers (usually Parsons and Blunstone) to drop deeper than usual to retrieve possession. Drake saw how well this ploy worked – thanks to the pace and work-rate of his two little flankers – and after a while asked them to drop back even deeper, which had the effect of completely losing their markers. Joker Parsons is said to have responded to these tactics by asking if Drake now wanted them to start taking goal-kicks too?

Chelsea certainly endured some physical battles during 1954-55, particularly against northern sides like Bolton. Jim Lewis, the amateur forward and scorer of some key goals, said Drake was as guilty as anyone in enforcing 'hard tactics'. He also recalled 'sledging' from an opposition defender who accused amateur players like Lewis of keeping decent professionals out of work. Lewis bravely told this notorious 'hard man' to keep his views to himself, only to earn himself a nasty injury for his trouble. Chelsea knew how to dish it out, too, of course, and Lewis recalled how manager Drake would often prime his experienced defender John Harris before a game over which players should be singled out for 'special treatment'.

It would be disrespectful to Drake's memory (he died in 1995), not to say a distortion of the truth, to suggest that Chelsea kicked their way to the title, however. There was no shortage of skill in the side and they chalked up a number of exciting wins and attacking displays during the campaign. In one wonderful fortnight approaching Christmas, for example, they hit twelve goals in three games, hammering high-flying Portsmouth, thrashing Aston Villa and, best of all, winning a 4-3 thriller at the home of reigning champions Wolves.

However, probably the most extraordinary game of all during 1954-55 was one which Chelsea lost. It took place in front of 56,000 astonished spectators at Stamford Bridge in October and saw Chelsea finish the ninety minutes empty-handed, despite scoring five goals, three of which represented a sensational hat-trick by debutant Seamus O'Connell.

Manchester United came out on top by 6-5, resisting enormous late pressure from the Blues to maintain their place at the top of the League. At that point, Chelsea, the great entertainers, were halfway down the table and looking anything but potential champions.

The eleven-goal thriller with Matt Busby's boys came during a run of four successive autumn defeats which saw Chelsea drop to twelfth. They had gone six successive home matches without a win – dating back to August – and Drake decided that desperate changes were required to halt the slump. Four players were axed, including Ron Greenwood, an intelligent and unflappable centre-half then in his thirties. He was replaced by a raw young defender who had been waiting patiently in the wings for his big chance. This was big Stan Wicks, twenty-six, a £10,500 signing from Drake's former team, Reading, nine months earlier. Wicks would soon establish himself as a regular in the side and catch the eye of those entrusted with selecting FA representative sides. The disgruntled Greenwood was allowed to move to Fulham.

Drake's re-shuffle at the beginning of November did the trick. The four straight losses were followed, first, by a 3-3 draw at Sunderland which featured a stunning goal by stand-in Les Stubbs, and then by a welcome home win over struggling Tottenham. Chelsea started like a train in that game with two goals in the first eight minutes. These two results restored confidence and Drake's men chalked up four successive wins to poke their noses into the top four by Christmas.

Chelsea's ruthless streak was evident at Burnden Park on New Year's Day, when five goals were hammered past injury-hit Bolton. The home crowd were left fuming over the visitors' no-nonsense tactics. Full-back Stan Willemse, in particular, so incensed the Wanderers' faithful with his fierce tackling and aggressive demeanour that he would receive hate-mail. One of his 'challenges' wrecked Harold Hassall's knee, the England inside-forward being rushed to hospital and ultimately having to quit the game. Afterwards, Ted Drake tried to defuse the situation, claiming that Willemse had been nowhere near the incident. Hassall, however, confirmed he had clashed with Willemse, although he graciously did not blame the Chelsea man for the 'tangle of legs' that prompted his career-ending injury.

Looking through the names who wore Chelsea's blue that season, it is clear that many of the key players were low-key signings made by the astute Drake. Stan Wicks, for example, blossomed after replacing Ron Greenwood in central defence, and Seamus O'Connell – who had been on amateur forms since the summer of 1954 – came in to do a fine job. O'Connell hailed from a wealthy cattle farming family in the north-east and was not keen to turn professional. His phenomenal debut against Manchester Untied left his manager not knowing whether to celebrate the player's hat-trick, or blast a defence which had conceded six goals at the other end.

One player who developed into a vital cog in Chelsea's team that season was full-back Sillett. Signed from Southampton for £13,000 in 1953, he was not initially a regular, due to National Service commitments. Sillett shared the No 2 shirt with veteran John Harris early in 1954-55, but by the end of the campaign he was an indispensable part of the team, his displays even winning praise from wing wizard Stan Matthews, who knew a thing or two about full-backs. Sillett emerged as skipper of the Young England side and would later win full caps.

The side that lifted the title was not expensively assembled or bursting with top-level pedigree. This was a squad made up of bargain buys and lower division experience, blended by Drake with the best of the talent he had inherited on his arrival at Chelsea in the summer of 1952. As well as Wicks and Sillett, Drake had raided the lower divisions for Johnny McNichol (from Brighton), Frank Blunstone (Crewe), Les Stubbs (Southend), not forgetting non-league amateurs Derek Saunders, Jim Lewis and O'Connell. However, Drake's skipper and top-scorer was the tried and trusted England centre-forward Roy Bentley, a classy performer who was effectively the manager's representative on the pitch. Drake trusted Bentley, who repaid the confidence shown in him.

Bentley believed Drake had taken an inconsistent side by the scruff, changing attitudes, outlook, and day-to-day training. With assistant secretary John Battersby promoted to handle the burden of administration, Drake – unlike his predecessors – was free to concentrate on team affairs. He effectively became one of the country's first 'tracksuit managers'. The players generally responded positively to Drake: 'He pepped up our training. Lap running can become extremely monotonous, but Ted gave us a ball and threw an entirely different light on this seemingly arduous job of work,' said Bentley.

At the start of the season, the press had predictably written off Chelsea's championship prospects, suggesting they were a better bet in the FA Cup. Chelsea's players and supporters in the main concurred with that view, but Drake always insisted his ambitions lay in the League and not the Cup. Bentley caught Drake's positive mood, telling *The People*: 'Wondering how near to the bottom we will finish is old stuff. Nowadys all we think of is how near the top we will be.'

As the possibility of the championship coming to Stamford Bridge became ever more probable during the spring of 1955, the astonishment of press and public alike was reflected by *Soccer Star* magazine: 'Fifty years without a single honour. Nothing but ridicule from chalk-faced comedians. An eternally empty sideboard. That's the Chelsea history for you.'

Sillett's penalty winner against Wolves at Easter and the subsequent sewing up of the League title meant a great many people had to eat their words. As Britain emerged from post-War austerity, Chelsea's success after fifty trophy-less years presented a splash of colour for an English football scene that was feeling rather sorry for itself after the recent lessons dished out to the national team by the Hungarians.

By the mid-1950s reconstruction from the destruction of war was well under way in London and elsewhere, rationing was easing, and a sense of optimism echoed through society. The rise of rock'n'roll music gathered momentum and life was a lot more colourful for the new generation of so-called 'teenagers'.

When Ted Drake, close to tears, stood clutching a microphone in the Main Stand at Stamford Bridge just before 5pm on St George's Day 1955, and declared this the happiest day of his life, the thousands of joyful supporters congregated below certainly felt they'd never had it so good. This book tells the story of how Chelsea reached that pinnacle – and what happened in the years immediately afterwards.

Chapter 1

FOUNDATIONS

(1905-1952)

Chelsea players have always been a colourful bunch. In the old days there were fellows like Fatty Foulke, a twenty-two-stone goalkeeper, and lanky Benjamin Baker, an Olympic high-jumper. For a while, even the famous music hall comedian George Robey was on the club's playing staff. Nowadays, the dressing room is a multi-lingual meeting place for mega-millionaires.

Over the course of 100 years, one suspects, more unusual footballing characters have passed through the doors of Stamford Bridge than of most other football clubs.

Life for Chelsea fans has always been a series of peaks and troughs; frustrating but never dull. Formed in 1905, the club did not win a single major trophy in its first fifty years despite vast crowd support and wealthy backers. Nevertheless, the eternal annual struggle to win something, anything, was in itself incentive for the supporters to keep coming back for more. Cavernous Stamford Bridge was home to West London's heroic failures, a major club who majored in under-achievement.

For half a century the prevailing wisdom was that 'Chelsea will never win anything – they're just Chelsea'. Northern folk dismissed them as a 'Fancy Dan' team with no substance. Fellow London clubs despised their shallow show-biz glamour. Neutrals regarded them as a harmless 'music hall' outfit. Even Chelsea's own fans developed low expectation-levels.

And then, for a short but momentous period in the early-to-mid 1950s, all that changed. A new manager, former England centre-forward Ted Drake, breezed into the Bridge on a one-man mission to give this eccentric football club a bit of backbone. Under Drake's command, Chelsea were soon fielding a team prepared to get stuck in and toil, week in and week out. England's Roy Bentley was appointed to skipper a bunch of players who famously knew how to 'get their retaliation in first' – but, crucially, who also possessed the footballing talent to go with their ruthless streak.

The outcome was a wholly unexpected victory in the race for the 1954-55 League Championship. Football folk couldn't believe it, least of all the glitterati types who populated Chelsea's main stand. Inevitably, this cut-price team's wonderful achievement was done in true Chelsea fashion, with a low points total, missed penalties galore, and a wobbly period in mid-season. And, perhaps even more predictably, the decline that followed the glory was swift.

Chelsea's fifty-year voyage to their first major triumph began as the result of a rich man's folly, shortly after the arrival of the twentieth century. Or, rather, two rich men's folly. Joe and Gus Mears were the sons of Joseph Mears, one of London's major building contractors, and these two brothers dreamed about creating the capital's finest sports stadium.

By the end of 1904, the Mears brothers had taken control of Stamford Bridge. For twenty-seven years the stadium had functioned as the HQ of the London Athletics Club, staging national championships and hosting world-class runners like Alf Shrubb. The Mears also acquired some adjacent meadow and market-garden land. The ambitious pair planned to develop the site into a venue that could host major events like Cup finals and internationals.

They set to work with the help of renowned stadium architect, the Scot Archibald Leitch. His plans featured a 120-yard long stand on the East side which could accommodate 5,000 spectators with an enclosure in front. The other sides, as was customary, were open to the elements, and shaped like a vast bowl. Banking for terracing was created from thousands of tons of material excavated from Underground railway tunnels nearby. The capacity was originally planned to be 100,000, which would make it the second largest stadium in the country, behind Crystal Palace, the FA Cup final venue. The project included provision for a new cinder running track for London AC, who would be allowed to continue using the ground, but on a tenancy basis.

As work got under way, the brothers' next step was to approach Sir Henry Norris, chairman of nearby Southern League Fulham, offering him use of the premises for his team's home matches, at a rent of £1,500 per year. To the Mears' surprise, the offer was declined. Fulham – having used twelve grounds in twenty-five years – were by now developing Craven Cottage as their permanent home.

With no major football club to occupy their huge arena, the disappointed Mears brothers considered selling Stamford Bridge to the Great Western Railway, but were dissuaded by business associate Jack Parker, an official of London AC. The astute Parker urged Gus and Joe to stick with their original plans, and to create a brand new football club of their own to occupy the site.

Geographically speaking, Stamford Bridge stood in Fulham territory, but as that name was already taken, some hard thinking had to be done regarding a name for the new club. Suggestions included Walham Green, Stamford Bridge, Kensington, and even London FC. Eventually neighbouring Chelsea was chosen to provide the identity and an application was hastily despatched to join the Southern League. Fulham and Tottenham Hotspur objected to the arrival of this brash and under-prepared new outfit, and the bid was thrown out. Undeterred, influence was exerted upon the Football League, which was expanding to forty clubs for the 1905-06 season. Following a meeting at the Tavistock Hotel in central London in May 1905, the new Chelsea FC was granted a place in the Second Division, along with other newcomers Hull, Leeds, Stockport, and Clapton Orient.

John Tait Robertson, the twenty-eight-year-old former Glasgow Rangers and Scotland captain, was recruited as player-manager to hastily assemble a new team. Among his captures was Warwickshire cricketer Jimmy Windridge, a 'wizard of the dribble' who cost £190 from Small Heath. But Robertson's most famous signing was giant goalkeeper Willie Foulke – living proof that quantity could be more important than quality in those days. A heavyweight in every sense, the colourful Foulke had won England caps during his time at Sheffield United, but was by now well past his best.

As a shot-stopper, however, he was still up there with the best. He could pick the ball up with one hand and clear great distances when punching away crosses. His fiery temper had, in the past, seen him snap crossbars and hurl opponents head first into the mud, but his main limitation was, shall we say, a lack of mobility. Manager Robertson made him captain, and introduced ball-boys for the first time at a football ground, essentially to collect stray balls for his ponderous custodian. The idea of ball-boys soon caught on at other grounds too.

The braver, or more foolhardy, of Foulke's teammates would, during training, tease Willie about his bulk. If Foulke was feeling energetic he would punish such banter by sitting on the man responsible until he apologised. One of Robertson's little psychological ploys was to ensure his smallest players ran out onto the pitch alongside Foulke, purely to accentuate his size and intimidate opponents. It worked against Burton Albion in that first season, for they missed two penalties, unable to squeeze the ball through the small amount of space offered between Foulke and the goalposts on either side.

After his career in football was over, the big man fell on hard times and was reduced to working beside the donkey rides on Blackpool pleasure beach as a 'Beat the Goalie' sideshow (one penny a go, threepence if you scored). Sadly, the bracing air contributed to his catching pneumonia and Foulke died aged just forty-two. Brian Mears, later to become chairman of Chelsea, pinpoints Foulke's arrival in 1905 as proof that the club were 'show-biz, right from day one'.

Foulke kept a batch of clean sheets in Chelsea's historic first season and only conceded twenty-seven goals in thirty-four Division Two games. It helped the team finish third. The opening game had been at fellow newcomers Stockport on 1st September, 1905, and ended in a 0-1 defeat, despite a penalty save by Foulke. A week later, at Blackpool, manager Robertson scored the club's first goal in a 1-0 win. The first home game was a midweek friendly which saw Liverpool beaten 4-0 in front of 6,000.

Admission to the terraces in those early days was sixpence, with the enclosure one shilling, and 1s 6d for the grandstand. A season ticket cost a guinea, half-price for women. The team sported light blue shirts and white shorts, and the club adopted the nickname 'The Pensioners', in recognition of the old soldiers occupying the famous Royal Hospital nearby. Alternative nicknames such as The Little Strangers, The Chelsea Chinamen, The Buns, and The Cherubs had all been rejected.

Chelsea attempted to build on their impressive start by recruiting a youthful scoring sensation called George Hilsdon from West Ham. In his first game, at home to Glossop, he hit five in a 9-2 win. His goals earned him international recognition and the soubriquet 'The Gatling Gunner'. Nearly 100 years after his debut he still looked down on Stamford Bridge, via a moulding of his image attached to a weather vane. He bagged twenty-seven goals in 1906-07 as Chelsea romped to promotion into Division One, finishing second, nine points clear of their nearest challenger.

Near the end of that season the club staged a benefit game for the widow of coach Jimmy Miller, who had died at Christmas 1906. The opposition XI were assembled by famous music hall comedian George Robey. Chelsea were so impressed by the lively Robey's display (he scored in his side's 3-0 win), that they signed him on amateur forms. Robey was now thirty-seven, but was no mean performer, and in earlier years had turned out for Millwall reserves.

Signing up Britain's top variety star strengthened Chelsea's links with the world of show-business. Although he failed to make the first team, Robey's name carried PR value and also attracted other household names to the terraces. Chelsea's reputation as an unpredictable and sometimes frustrating team would provide Robey and fellow comedians with plenty of material for their acts over the years.

Player-manager Robertson left Stamford Bridge towards the end of the promotion season to join Glossop. His post remained vacant for some weeks until Lincoln manager and former Scottish international defender David Calderhead arrived. Calderhead had impressed the Chelsea directors only a month or two earlier by leading his Red Imps side to a surprise FA Cup victory at Stamford Bridge.

Calderhead would ultimately become Chelsea's longest-serving boss, working as secretary-manager from 1907 to 1933 and winning a Football League Long Service award. Chelsea enjoyed an up-and-down existence during the Calderhead years. Relegation from Division One came in 1910 despite big cash outlays on new players, but within a year the club battled to its first FA Cup semi-final, losing 0-3 to Newcastle. Promotion back to the top flight followed in 1912, only for Calderhead's men to drop back again three years later.

The onset of the 1914-18 War saw leading Chelsea players Vivian 'VJ' Woodward and Bob Whittingham depart to join the 'Footballers' Battalion' (the 17th Middlesex regiment). To fill the void, Chelsea enticed players from Scotland. The team competed in the London Combination, winning this makeshift league in 1915 and 1918. They also reached the wartime cup final of 1915, but were defeated 0-3 by Sheffield United. Pre-Great War England star Woodward was available for the final, but generously insisted that Bob Thomson keep his place as a reward for his many wartime goals for the club. Sadly, Thomson was unable to replay the gesture with a goal. Thomson was an ace marksman, despite having only one eye. When asked how he could hit the target so often he liked to reply: 'I just close my eye and play from memory.'

Despite finishing second-from-bottom in 1914-15, Chelsea avoided relegation when football resumed in 1919-20, thanks only to the League's expansion. The top division was enlarged from twenty to twenty-two clubs. Having 'escaped' relegation, they promptly finished third and reached the FA Cup semi-final. Had they not been knocked out by Aston Villa, Chelsea would have presented the FA with a problem, for the final was scheduled for Stamford Bridge, and the rules only allowed for neutral venues. The only other ground big enough was Crystal Palace, but that had been requisitioned by the War Office. In fact, Stamford Bridge staged two more Cup finals before Wembley took over in 1923.

A popular Chelsea player of this era was centre-forward Jack Cock, remembered for his fine features and his tenor voice, not to mention his athleticism and spectacular goals. On retiring from football he turned to, you've guessed it, music hall.

Olympic high jumper and part-time goalkeeper Howard Benjamin-Baker was on Chelsea's books, but this remarkable character's various sporting commitments often restricted his appearances. The fans loved him for his extrovert antics. In November 1920 he dashed from his goal and insisted on taking a penalty. He duly scored, but a later attempt from the spot was saved and he had to sprint back to his goal to prevent the opposition scoring from the clearance. As well as representing his country in the 1912 and 1920 Olympics, this versatile sportsman also excelled at tennis, water polo and high-diving.

A club record seven successive wins left Chelsea ninth in 1921-22, but a slump set in and relegation followed in 1924. Key man around this time was nimble-footed Andy Wilson, who brushed off a wartime injury to his arm to skipper the side. His splendid ball control and play-making skills saw him set up goals galore for others, as well as bagging a healthy number himself.

During the so-called jazz age of the 1920s, Chelsea were marooned in the Second Division, regularly missing promotion by just a few points. Opponents included the likes of Gateshead and Darlington, but gates remained high. The 1924-25 season began on a sad note when live-wire half-back Tommy Meehan, a £3,300 buy from Manchester United, died following an illness. He left a large family and the FA and other clubs sent donations to help provide for them.

A final placing of ninth in Division Two at the end of 1928-29 would represent the lowest finish in the club's first seventy years. Following the final game of this campaign – a 2-1 home win over Reading, refereed by Stanley Rous – the club set off on a ground-breaking six-week tour of South America. Chelsea tackled nine 'friendly' games in Argentina, Brazil and Uruguay, winning four and losing three. The welcome was cordial in Argentina, who were then on good terms with Britain. On the same day that Racing Club of Buenos Aires thrashed Chelsea 4-0, the British Government announced that the Argentine capital would stage the British Empire Industries Fair, the greatest exhibition ever staged in the southern hemisphere. Chelsea's tour was topped and tailed by seven-day trans-Atlantic voyages, which were regarded by club officials as an opportunity to foster team spirit.

Maybe it worked, because the following season, 1929-30, saw promotion achieved – although two defeats in the final three games almost messed things up. Division One status had been regained after six seasons and plans were made to improve Stamford Bridge in anticipation of bigger crowds. In the summer of 1930 the Shed End terraced area was erected. A vast bank behind the southern goal, it would soon become the favoured vantage point of Chelsea's most die-hard supporters.

Chelsea and Arsenal were the first English teams to use numbered shirts during the subsequent season, which saw Chelsea invest heavily in their playing squad and achieve a mid-table finish. The major transfer buy was pint-sized Scotland international Hughie Gallagher, signed from Newcastle for a record £10,000. A fiery character, Gallagher was a lethal finisher and accurate passer of the ball, who often incurred rough treatment from opponents. He would occasionally ask referees for a three-minute 'time out' to go off and try to calm down. Newcastle were said to have parted company because of his extravagant nightlife. Arriving in London, Gallagher settled into digs in Barons Court and his taste for socialising certainly did not diminish in this West End setting. He went on to enjoy four great years at Stamford Bridge, scoring eighty-one goals from 144 games, but off-field shenanigans ultimately led to his departure. Problems involving alcohol and family matters would ultimately lead to 'wee Hughie' taking his own life on a railway line.

Chelsea's other forward-line imports in 1930 were Alec Cheyne, costing £6,000 from Aberdeen, and Alec Jackson, known as 'The Gay Cavalier', for £8,500 from Huddersfield. The three new Scots teamed up with little Jackie Crawford, the team's practical joker, to form a potent forward line. Sadly the defence failed to play its part in 1931, and took the blame for calamitous defeats at the hands of Aston Villa (Pongo Waring hit four in a 3-6 defeat) and at Everton (where Dixie Dean hit five of Everton's seven).

Chelsea's team of the early 1930s featured fearless left-back and so-called 'Wembley Wizard' Tommy Law from Scotland. In some games the club was able to field nine internationals. Little Gallagher netted thirty goals in forty-one games during 1931-32. At the end of that season, Chelsea toured Germany, where enigmatic centre-half Peter O'Dowd announced he was unwell and unable to play. The management suspected he was malingering and this episode hastened his departure. He eventually signed for Valenciennes for £3,000, the first Englishman to command a fee from a French club.

Chelsea avoided relegation by just two points in 1932-33, after which long-serving manager Calderhead departed and was replaced by Leslie Knighton, who had produced winning teams at Bournemouth and Birmingham. Like his predecessor, Knighton's role was 'secretary-manager', with Jack Whitley in charge of day-to-day training. The new manager's first campaign in charge saw the Pensioners escape relegation by just a couple of points. The next four seasons saw the club hover around mid-table, well clear of relegation, but offering little in the way of excitement. Chelsea's reputation as a team that promised much but delivered little was becoming firmly established.

Vic Woodley was a popular and reliable figure in goal in the 1930s, and won nineteen caps for England. Another favourite was Irish forward Joe

Bambrick, who signed in December 1934 and is largely remembered for scoring six times on his international debut. In October 1935 a ground record of 82,905 was established for the visit of Arsenal, but a week later Chelsea were watched at Everton's Goodison Park by just 19,000 as Dixie Dean and Joe Mercer inspired the home side to a 5-1 win. The 1935-36 season ended on a sad note when founder Joseph Mears, chairman Claude Kirby, and assistant secretary Bert Palmer all passed away within a short period of time.

The 1938-39 season proved to be a watershed. Chelsea slumped to the nether regions of Division One and only survived the drop by one point, thanks to a late spurt. They enjoyed a lengthy Cup run, however, reaching the quarter-finals before being knocked out 0-1 at home by Grimsby. Billy Birrell, manager of QPR, was hired to replace Knighton in mid-1939 and is credited with being the instigator of the club's youth policy, which began to pay dividends after the 1939-45 War.

Meanwhile, a new stand at the northern end of the ground was constructed in 1939 to offer spectators greater protection from the elements. After a 0-1 defeat at Anfield in early September 1939, war was declared and League football suspended. A few weeks later the makeshift 'Football League South' was up and running, and clubs were permitted to use guest players. These interim matches entertained war-torn Britain until serious competition could resume.

A regular player during the war years was half-back Dick Foss, who would later take charge of Chelsea's pioneering youth scheme and is credited with developing internationals such as Greaves, Bonetti, Hudson and Osgood. Chelsea's only tangible successes from the War years saw them reach Wembley twice, defeated in the 1944 Football League South Cup final 0-2 by Charlton, but making amends a year later with a 2-0 triumph over Millwall.

Competitive football returned in 1946. Many talented footballers had lost the best years of their playing careers, but there was plenty of optimism at Stamford Bridge as manager Birrell made several important signings in time for the return of serious action. A popular performer in 1946-47 was the giant Swiss full-back Willi Steffen. A wartime fighter pilot who spoke six languages, Steffen was a practical joker, popular with colleagues and fans alike.

Defenders John Harris and Danny Winter arrived at the Bridge from Wolves and Bolton respectively, and inside-forward Len Goulden from West Ham, each costing £5,000. Winger Tommy Walker (later awarded an OBE) arrived from Hearts for £6,000, and West Ham goalkeeper Harry Medhurst replaced the ageing Woodley. But the most notable capture of all was England centre-forward Tommy Lawton, for a club record £11,500. Lawton was now twenty-six and theoretically at his peak, but of course he had not played competitive football for seven years.

Lawton's arrival generated huge publicity and his first appearance in blue enticed a massive crowd of 53,813 to Stamford Bridge for the visit of Birmingham City. Chelsea lost 2-3 but Lawton was an instant hit, scoring both goals. An even bigger occasion arrived three days later when a crowd approaching 100,000 squeezed in to witness the friendly against Moscow Dynamo, who were making their first public appearance on a well-publicised tour. Around 75,000 paid for entry, but it was clear thousands more had 'forced' their way in.

The mysterious Soviets' first surprise was their unusual Baltic-blue kit, complete with large white 'D' emblazoned on the chests. They then caused a fuss by presenting each Chelsea player with a bouquet. When the captains came together to toss up, Dynamo's Mikhail Semichastny did not understand a word of what referee Lt Cdr Clark was asking. He was more used to the Soviet method – selecting a folded paper which concealed the words 'kick off' or 'choice of ends'. It took some time for the coin-tossing procedure to be explained. The game's other main talking point was the referee, who allowed a late equaliser by Bobrov (to make it 3-3) which looked obviously offside. He had given the goal, he later explained, for 'diplomatic reasons'. So diplomatic that Tommy Lawton exploded with rage, unable to believe that diplomacy could be used as an excuse to fix a match, let alone deprive his team of their win bonus.

Dynamo's ground-breaking tour also saw them beat Cardiff 10-1 and Arsenal 4-3, and draw with Glasgow Rangers. Their four games attracted an aggregate of over a quarter of a million spectators. Football's post-War boom was evident for all to see, and there was a huge demand to see the exotic Soviets. The visitors were displeased, however, by the overly physical nature of the British game. They were shocked by the way centre-forwards routinely 'shoulder-charged' opponents off the ball. In turn, the British players were not too keen on the way the tourists regularly resorted to obstruction as a defensive tactic. The atmosphere of international goodwill manifest at the start of the Chelsea game had all but vanished a week or two later. The tourists were even accused of sneaking a twelfth player onto the pitch in the fog of Ibrox Park.

Writing in *The Tribune*, George Orwell suggested that sport was 'an unfailing source of ill-will', and cautioned against any reciprocal tour. Not long afterwards a stage show was introduced in Moscow which depicted the Dynamo team as incorruptible socialist heroes, bravely battling the wiles of the corrupt capitalists.

Nevertheless, the tour had lifted the spirits of war-weary football fans in Britain, and at their farewell gathering at The Scala Theatre, the visitors expressed thanks for their warm reception and stated their admiration for the London transport system. Manager Mikhail Yakushin said his side played in the 'socialist way', which involved players switching positions during games, creating a fluid style that often left British opponents floundering. One particular talking-point was the deep-lying centre-forward tactic, more of which later. The visitors' ideas were considered novel and potent, but by and large British football continued on its merry way long after the Soviets had returned home.

During 1946-47, the first competitive post-War season, Arctic conditions caused multiple cancellations that forced the season to extend to 14th June. Chelsea finished a disappointing fifteenth, although Lawton banged in thirty goals in thirty-nine games. He asked for time off after suffering food poisoning while on England duty, but Chelsea insisted he accompany them on an end-of-season tour to Scandinavia – an order that Lawton defied. Relations between player and club soured and within a few months Lawton had moved to Notts County (whose manager was a friend) despite counter-offers from bigger clubs. Chelsea fans were understandably furious.

Manager Birrell's own raids into the transfer market saw him pick up useful players like Ken Armstrong (Bradford Rovers), Bobby Campbell (Falkirk), Bill Dickson (Notts County), Hughie Billington and Bill Hughes (both Luton), and Eric Parsons (West Ham). The pacy Campbell scored twice on his 1947 debut and was a regular for six seasons, setting up goal-chances galore. The man with the unenviable task of stepping into Lawton's boots would be Roy Bentley, who cost £11,000 from Newcastle. Chelsea fans did not take to him at first, but Bentley soon changed their opinions and went on to become one of the most influential figures in the club's history.

In February 1948 Birrell's youth scheme was launched when a team of youngsters called Tudor Rose took to the pitch for the first time at Stamford Bridge. Effectively the Chelsea youth team, Tudor Rose would soon set up home beside the Welsh Harp reservoir in North London and the development of stars of the future was set in train. With hindsight, the first Tudor Rose game was a notable day in the club's history, although most old-timers remember this era for just one thing – the double disappointment in FA Cup semi-finals at the hands of Arsenal.

In 1950 and 1952 the club reached the last four of the FA Cup, and were paired with the Gunners on both occasions. Both ties required a replay and on both occasions the Gunners eventually triumphed, with

Freddie Cox among the scorers. It was hugely disappointing for Pensioners' fans, made worse by a poor League season in 1950-51, when relegation was only avoided the antiquated system of goal-average. Chelsea won their final game that season by 4-0 against Bolton, but there was an agonising wait to see if they were safe. Eventually it was calculated that they had survived by 0.44 of a goal, with the bottom three sides all locked together on thirty-two points.

At least the long-suffering fans could forget their woes by visiting a new attraction a short distance from Stamford Bridge, which opened a few days after the 1950-51 season ended. The Festival of Britain attracted more than eight million visitors that summer. Wartime hardships and shortages were now to be commemorated by a collective 'pat on the back' in the form of this Festival. Twenty-seven acres of war-blasted Victorian warehousing and backstreet industry had been cleared beside County Hall for a show that provided – for the first time in a dozen grim years – colour, light, innovation, flair, and the excitement of the new.

A few months later, shortly before Christmas 1951, under-achieving Chelsea missed a golden opportunity to sign a major young talent for free. The story goes that Bill Slater, a highly-rated young amateur from Blackpool, decided to move south to be near his girlfriend Marion, who happened to live in West London. Bill and Marion apparently studied a map of the metropolis, settled on Chelsea, and went along to knock on the club's office door.

Talking about the episode years later, Marion said that when a commissionaire opened the door, Bill said meekly that he'd come to see about the possibility of playing for Chelsea. Inevitably, the door started to close, but Bill quickly told the man he'd played for Blackpool in that year's Cup final. This did the trick and the pair were led into an office and introduced to a female member of staff. Bill told her he was a wing-half, but she was unimpressed and said Chelsea already had two good wing-halves – and promptly showed Bill and Marion the door! The rejected star then tried Brentford, who were only too happy to sign him up. Slater, of course, went on to enjoy a fine career with Wolves and England. Chelsea boss Birrell is said to have 'gone bananas' when he heard what had happened. The London *Evening Standard* even ran a cartoon of young Slater in a Santa Claus hat with the caption: 'A Christmas present for Brentford.'

Poor Birrell. Events like this must have helped persuade him that the time was right to reach for his pipe and slippers and slip quietly into retirement. His contract was due to expire in June 1952, and he was content for the Chelsea directors to begin the search for a new manager. Ultimately, their choice would prove inspired.

Chapter 2

DRAKE TAKES THE HELM

(May 1952 – June 1954)

With manager Billy Birrell looking forward to retirement in May 1952, the Chelsea directors sounded out Division Three (South) promotion-chasers Reading about taking their popular young manager Ted Drake.

Drake was flattered by the interest, but not keen to rush into a new job without assurances about his new employers' level of ambition. It would be some time before agreement was reached and a contract signed. Drake undertook private research by inviting established Chelsea players Roy Bentley and John Harris to join him on the golf course, where he quizzed them about life behind the scenes at the Bridge.

Speculation ended when his appointment was announced on Saturday, 30th April 1952 – the day of the penultimate match of the 1951-52 season – which brought a 0-2 home defeat by Spurs. Drake, a thirty-nine-year-old former England centre-forward, started his new job in the summer and found life very different to that at Elm Park, where he had guided Reading to second place, behind promoted Plymouth.

Roy Bentley, Chelsea's leading scorer over the three campaigns before Drake's arrival, and one of the new manager's successors in the England No 9 shirt, expressed delight at the appointment. Looking back, he reckons Drake was 'the greatest thing that could have happened to the club', with better training methods introduced and coaching more professionally organised. In Bentley's view, the players became more focused and played like a real team. Drake's early chats with players and press saw him dismiss the view that Chelsea were 'a Cup side'. Instead he talked in terms of creating a League-winning outfit within three years.

One question that preoccupied Drake at once was the club's image. He hated the nickname 'Pensioners' and was also dismissive of the club's long-established ties to showbusiness. Bentley recalled: 'Ted didn't like the reputation the club had as a theatre stars' Saturday afternoon hangout. Dickie Attenborough came to train with the players once, but he was different as he has always remained loyal to the club.' Drake made it clear he wanted the Pensioner image replaced by something grittier. He had the club badge changed to one featuring a roaring lion motif. From that point, the Pensioners' image faded, and although no alternative nickname was formally adopted, the mundane 'Blues' became the popular choice by force of habit. Drake heralded the start of a new era by appealing in his first programme notes for fans to be more committed. They had a reputation for sportsmanship and for applauding skill by the opposition – but Drake demanded less generosity and greater hostility. He hoped to transform Stamford Bridge into a place the opposition feared.

But his most important task was to create a side that would play as a team and not as a collection of individuals. Bentley recalls that Drake set strict parameters when looking for new talent. The manager often lost interest in a player who was not married, and who was therefore denied the benefits of a stable home life. Drake worked on getting certain of his inherited players to change their ways too, if he spotted anything unprofessional in their off-field behaviour. He made use of Bentley's sense and experience and the pair would spend hours together, discussing the forthcoming game and the behaviour of other players. Drake also became known as one of the first managers to put on training gear and join in on the training field.

Leading football writer Brian Glanville noticed a change in Drake after he arrived at Stamford Bridge. He was transformed from the roistering, jesting extrovert who'd managed Reading, into a more subdued and pinstriped figure at Chelsea. Drake seemed intent on building a team at Stamford Bridge that was no longer volatile but functional.

So it was all-change at Chelsea in 1952, and indeed in Britain in general. Probably the most important development nationally was the easing of the country's economic plight. It may have been something of an illusion, but the message from Whitehall was that full employment with no inflation had been achieved. Loose change was jangling in trouser pockets again, signalling the emergence of youth culture. James Dean and Marlon Brando were the new anti-heroes, and the advent of TV – hastened by the demand to watch the Coronation of Queen Elizabeth II in 1953 – had a major effect on lifestyle. With hindsight it is clear that English soccer stood in bleak contrast to the social and technological advancement that surrounded it. Crowds continued to fall after peaking in 1948-49, and on the international scene England's outdated play would soon be exposed in humiliating fashion.

The domestic game clearly needed some dynamic young managers to instil new ideas and Drake looked like he was made of the right stuff. But who exactly was this determined young man who was kicking open doors at the Bridge to allow the winds of change to whistle through?

Drake had been the quintessential English centre-forward before the 1939-45 war – big, strong, quick and fearless. After promising displays as a teenager with local non-leaguers Winchester, he joined Southampton, then a mid-table Second Division outfit, in 1931. He cracked a hat-trick on his debut and went on to register forty-eight goals in seventy-two matches for The Saints.

Following the death of legendary Arsenal boss Herbert Chapman, George Allison was put in charge at Highbury. His first signing was Drake, who cost £6,000 in March 1934. In the last ten games of that season Drake hit seven goals to help clinch the championship, but had not been in the side long enough to qualify for a medal. In his first full season with the Gunners, Drake hit a record forty-two goals in forty-one League appearances. In four of these matches he bagged a foursome, and one of those was against Chelsea. His goals ensured that Arsenal clinched a third consecutive League Championship in 1935. A few months later he smashed another record, scoring all seven of Arsenal's goals in a 7-1 demolition of Aston Villa at Villa Park. He is said to have had nine scoring chances in that game, with one of the 'failures' hitting the bar and the other producing a brilliant save. The Villa players later cleaned the match ball and presented it to him, bearing the message 'For you lad – and there's no hard feelings'.

Apart from his prolific scoring, Drake was also known for his keen sense of humour. In one tactics talk at Arsenal, manager Allison improvised by using eleven bottles of lemonade to represent players. Having left the room briefly, Allison was told on his return by a serious looking Drake: 'The centre-forward's drunk, Mr Allison.' And so he was, or rather had been ... by Ted!

Like many top players of the era, Drake's career was curtailed by the War, but in addition to service as an RAF flight-lieutenant, he turned out in Arsenal colours in 128 wartime games and scored eighty-six goals. Sadly, at Reading, he damaged his spine in a bad fall and was forced to quit. He had just passed thirty but had looked set for several more seasons at the top. His tally was a remarkable 124 goals in 168 (peacetime) League appearances, plus twelve in fourteen FA Cup-ties, and three in two Charity Shield appearances. His career honours included two championship medals, an FA Cup winners medal, and five England caps. Away from football he played cricket for Hampshire and once caught Arsenal teammate Joe Hulme, who was batting for Middlesex. Drake's sporting talents also extended to golf, and after joining Chelsea he established a regular Monday routine of a round or two with fellow London club managers Jimmy Seed and Frank Osborne.

With his playing days behind him, Drake had become manager of non-league Hendon in 1946 before joining Reading a year later. He achieved a trio of top-three positions with Reading, and their reserve side shocked bigger clubs by winning the Football Combination. A Reading FC statistician recently calculated that in terms of games won, Drake is the club's most successful manager ever. A move to a bigger club became inevitable and Chelsea won the race for his services in 1952.

One of the new manager's first moves was to dispense with little Scottish inside-forward Jimmy Leadbetter, who went to Brighton in part-exchange for the Seagulls' skipper Johnny McNichol. Drake also had a confidence-boosting chat with winger Eric Parsons, who had been going through a bad patch before Drake's arrival. The manager said he had complete faith in the player and insisted he forget his recent poor form. The pep-talk worked wonders.

Drake's first match in charge at Chelsea came a week after his fortieth birthday. It kicked off the 1952-53 season with a 0-2 defeat at Old Trafford. Drake set about scouring the lower leagues for talent, which was just as well, for Chelsea started badly and got worse. Although they chalked up some notable wins at home, away results were abysmal. The the first victory on their travels did not arrive until mid-March, at Tottenham, after seventeen winless trips.

Drake raided smaller clubs for players like McNichol, Les Stubbs from Southend and, perhaps his most inspired acquisition of all, eighteen-year-old winger Frank Blunstone from Crewe. Blunstone arrived in February 1953 for a bargain £7,000. That year also saw the introduction of Southampton full-back Peter Sillett (his brother John followed less than a year later) and Derek Saunders, red-haired and reliable, a quietly effective left-half, from amateurs Walthamstow Avenue. The same East London club also provided British Olympic international winger Jim Lewis. Seamus O'Connell, another exciting amateur attacker, was signed up while remaining on Bishop Auckland's books.

Centre-half Ron Greenwood, who had played for Chelsea during the War, rejoined after spells with Bradford and Brentford. Drake also signed former Reading centre-half Stan Wicks and Clyde keeper Charlie 'Chick' Thomson. Of those players he had inherited on arrival, Drake ultimately kept faith with three – full-back Stan Willemse, veteran defender John Harris and centre-forward Roy Bentley. One by one the others fell by the wayside as Drake moulded the team to his liking.

New winger Blunstone recalled Drake's management style as a mix of calm and storm, with the occasional teacup being flung in the dressing room on occasions when things were going badly. Drake would turn up to watch a training session in suit and shiny leather shoes, but would not hesitate to cake them in mud if he felt the need to demonstrate a thing or two. Drake could not be described as a master tactician, according to Blunstone: 'There weren't really many tactics in those days. Me and Parsons just had to beat the full-back, get to the by-line and pull a good cross back, and we were always encouraged to take people on.'

Although he had been a 'tracksuit manager' in his early days at Chelsea, Drake's daily involvement on the training field was curtailed by continuing back-pain, a legacy from the injury that ended his playing days. Bentley recalled that Drake would quietly slip away to have physio-therapy nearly every day at the ground, but kept quiet about it, never letting on about the pain he was in.

Drake's first winter as a top-flight manager coincided with the capital suffering the worst smog (a health-threatening combination of smoke and fog that has thankfully disappeared from our weather) ever known. Just after Christmas 1952 conditions deteriorated to such an extent that fewer than 18,000 groped their way to Stamford Bridge to 'see' a goalless draw with Stoke. The mother of all 'pea-soupers' meant spectators could hardly see their hands in front of their faces. Reportedly, Royal Albert Hall concert audiences were unable to see the orchestra from the stalls. Water condensing on smoke from coal fires was blamed, and although anti-smog masks were issued, more than 2,000 Londoners perished around this time due to respiratory problems.

Smog or no smog, Drake's first season ended with Chelsea struggling from start to finish and escaping relegation by just two points. The final day's 3-1 win over fellow strugglers Manchester City proved decisive. As he continued his rebuilding programme, Drake must have cast envious eyes toward Old Trafford, where Matt Busby was on a similar mission with his ageing reigning champions. Busby had some wonderful teenage talent at his disposal and introduced players like Duncan Edwards, David Pegg and Dennis Viollet. The phrase 'The Busby Babes' was born at this point and Drake was known to watch keenly the way Busby pragmatically dismantled a title-winning side to make way for youth.

Chelsea's battle to steer clear of the drop in 1953 was hardly helped by a marathon FA Cup fourth round battle with West Brom. It needed four matches and 420 minutes of action before the sides could be separated. Chelsea finally prevailed in the third replay, at Highbury, by 4-0. Referee that day was Yorkshireman Arthur Ellis, who would later find fame as an adjudicator on TV's It's A Knockout. The Cup marathon took its toll and three days later a leg-weary Chelsea were knocked out at the fifth-round stage, hammered 0-4 at home by Birmingham.

The Government increased Entertainment Tax on football for 1952-53 and raised admission fees by threepence to one shilling and ninepence.

This, combined with the increasing popularity of TV, saw the post-War attendance boom cool off. Gates across the country fell by about two million. Crowd sizes at Stamford Bridge were again mixed, with bumper turnouts in excess of 60,000 for the visits of Wolves, Tottenham, and Arsenal, but fewer than 18,000 to see Stoke and Liverpool. The worst attended games were inevitably the midweek afternoon fixtures brought about by Saturday postponements. The FA still refused to permit the use of floodlights at competitive games, although Arsenal and Southampton both staged friendlies under lights, which caught the public imagination and were hailed a big success. It looked to be only be a matter of time before the FA would relent on this issue.

February 1953 proved to be a hectic month for Chelsea, with eight games played and just one victory recorded. However, Drake's frustration at this poor return was nothing compared to that endured by Sheffield Wednesday's Derek Dooley, who broke his leg in a collision with the Preston goalkeeper. A gash sustained earlier became infected, leading to gangrene and then amputation. The football world was shocked by this dreadful end to a footballer's career.

Only two First Division sides scored fewer goals than Chelsea during 1952-53, but with relegation avoided by a whisker, Drake was convinced his team's fortunes could only improve the following season.

Sure enough, 1953-54 saw major improvements in form and Chelsea rose to a finishing position of eighth, their best in eighteen years. One of the season's highlights was a 4-2 win over champions-elect Wolves at Stamford Bridge. Goals by Bentley (two), Stubbs and Eric Parsons sank Stan Cullis's side. Chelsea looked fresh and lively following a mid-season mini-break in Switzerland, which was preparing to host the 1954 World Cup. The win was hugely satisfying for Drake, and provided some measure of revenge for the 1-8 hammering suffered at Molineux earlier in the season, which had even featured a touchline bust-up between the two managers. Although Wolves' cause was helped that day by injuries to two Chelsea men, the overall effect of the thrashing was to prompt Drake into a number of team changes, which ushered in a steady improvement in form.

For Chelsea fans, a result like that at Molineux was momentarily stunning, but not the signal to sink into a black depression. Most of those who got their Saturday afternoon entertainment at Stamford Bridge were well used to ups and downs and took defeat philosophically. But this lack of a winning mentality irritated Drake, whose priority was victory, not entertainment. It would take a few years before the attitude of most Chelsea fans changed in tune with that of the manager.

At this time, Tony Banks – who would grow up to become an MP and government minister – was a keen young fan in short trousers, devoted to the Chelsea cause. Asked about the attitude and general demeanour of the fans back in the 1950s, he said he couldn't remember any barracking of players and described the era as 'a gentler time'. This is affirmed by writer Geoffrey Gover in his book *Explaining English Character*, in which he describes the behaviour of huge early 1950s football crowds as 'orderly as church meetings'.

Tony Banks says: 'There was always plenty of good natured banter going on, for this was an innocent age. Because of the layout of Stamford Bridge, you didn't get the crowd baying at a player or breathing down his neck. However, I do remember one forward, Bobby Campbell [1947-54], who got a bit of stick and was given the nickname Lino, for he was always on the floor.'

Another young fan, John Root, now living in Texas, explained that he began supporting Chelsea after his pal's dad – a publican at the corner of Lower Sloane Street and Pimlico Road – took them to a match and stood them against the front fence at the Shed end. Root told the Chelsea official website: 'I still remember the old east stand with the words Chelsea Football Club painted in giant letters on the side of the stand. Of course there was no west stand in those days, just what seemed like acres and acres of terraces. I became a regular at the Boys Entrance to home games. As I remember, I got in for sixpence and spent another threepence on a programme. With tube fare from Victoria included, I could have a great Saturday afternoon for about 1s 3d. Early favourites of mine, besides Tommy Lawton, were Harry Medhurst in goal, Ken Armstrong and, of course, Roy Bentley. I still believe that the greatest goal I ever saw in person was by Bentley against Manchester United. Billy Gray had gone down the right wing, towards the north end, and executed a perfect back-heel pass. Bentley connected just outside the area, as I recall, and I remember that it appeared he was running back for the ensuing kick-off with his hands in the air in celebration even before the ball was in the net! Shortly after that my parents and I emigrated to the States, and I've lived here ever since, but I've never lost my enthusiasm for Chelsea.'

While things were beginning to look up for Chelsea in late 1953, the English game in general suffered a body-blow when the Hungarian national team descended on Wembley and inflicted a 6-3 defeat, ruthlessly exposing shortcomings in the home side. Six months later they proved it was no flash in the pan, winning the return 7-1 in Budapest.

For England, a revolution was demanded, but on the domestic front Chelsea fans were comforted by signs of better things to come from their side. By the end of his second season, Drake was a far happier man than he had been at the end of his first. Roy Bentley recalls that Drake's work was beginning to pay off: 'We all felt we were becoming a good side.' Bentley's role as Drake's 'lieutenant' was proving to be a fruitful relationship and the manager appreciated having him around to bounce ideas off, and as a means of liaising with the players. For his part, Bentley was playing the best football of his life, despite his thirtieth birthday looming in May 1954.

Bristolian Bentley had an interesting background. Having left school in 1938 aged fourteen, he had signed as a Bristol Rovers groundstaff boy for £1 10s per week. His role involved odd jobs around the ground, with hardly any football. When the cash-strapped club asked all players to take a pay cut, Bentley found himself down to ten shillings a week and, on his father's advice, switched to neighbours Bristol City, who were happy to have him. When war broke out in 1939, many City players were called into the armed forces, leaving the club short on man-power. It meant Bentley got an early first-team chance:

'All of a sudden I was getting the best football education a lad could get,' he recalled. As a sixteen-year-old playing on the wing he was able to learn from the internationals who guested for City, and recalled picking up vital 'tricks of the trade' from the likes of Billy Mitchell, an Irish international wing-half, who taught him how to look after himself on the pitch. Worried that they might lose Bentley when he was called up to join the Navy, City offered him a contract before his seventeenth birthday. In his last game before setting sail, a notorious Cardiff City full-back broke Bentley's ankle in response to constantly being outstripped by the young upstart. Bentley missed his ship as a result, and was stunned to learn later that the ship in question had been attacked by the Germans on its journey without him.

While home on leave in 1946, Bentley shone against Brentford in a Cup-tie and impressed a watching Newcastle scout. Without the player's knowledge, an £8,500 transfer deal was agreed. Bentley went off with Bristol City to tour Scandinavia and was mystified by never being picked for the starting eleven. The penny dropped when he was finally told he would be joining one of Europe's top forward lines at St James' Park – Jackie Milburn, Charlie Wayman, Len Shackleton, and Tommy Pearson.

This dream move did not work out for the West Country lad, however, even though he did manage twenty-two goals in the Magpies' black and white. Illness affected his form and within eighteen months he headed south again, this time to Chelsea for £12,500. Looking back, Bentley scoffs at the press speculation, which blamed his move from Newcastle on a row stemming from a dirty bath in his Geordie digs. 'Truth is I was very unwell,' he said. 'I was putting so much energy into training that I was running on empty and was diagnosed with the onset of consumption – tuberculosis as they now call it. I'd lost so much weight that the League's own doctor was called in and he was concerned enough to demand I be sent away to somewhere warmer to recuperate. The club decided to sell me for my own sake.'

Away from chilly Tyneside, Bentley passed a medical at Chelsea but found the southern fans not quite as welcoming as the warmer weather: 'I took a while to adjust when I first came to Chelsea and I remember the first time I ran out of the tunnel, one particular bloke said "Oy Bentley you're useless, get back to Newcastle". Later on, when things got better I got my own back by always pulling a sour face at him as I went down the tunnel. Then, years later at Ascot, I was told the bloke had stopped going after the first time I did it, so for years I must have been pulling this face at someone else!

'After I joined, the atmosphere of the big crowds hit you in the face as you ran out. Now, the atmosphere is very different, it seems to come down on you from the high stands, because there's not the open sky like there used to be back then. The pitch wasn't flat then either, and the water would run away off to the corners as it was higher in the middle. Two players could lie down on either side of the penalty area near the touchline and they wouldn't be able to see each other – that's how sloping it was.'

Although Chelsea urgently needed a consistent goalscorer to step into Tommy Lawton's boots, Billy Birrell gave Bentley plenty of time to capture his form following his illness. His early games were a disappointment and he was soon rested. But near the end of 1947-48 his luck changed. Forward Jimmy Bowie was injured in an accident with a snooker table and Bentley was called up to replace him. He scored for the first time in a Chelsea shirt and his general play earned approval. Soon afterwards he was switched from inside-right to centre-forward and never looked back, becoming leading scorer for the seven subsequent seasons.

To the glee of Chelsea fans, England manager Walter Winterbottom and his selection committee at last picked Bentley in May 1949. In his second England appearance, Bentley scored the winner against Scotland at Hampden, thus helping England qualify for the World Cup finals in Brazil. The Home International tournament had been nominated as a qualifying zone in its own right. Shortly afterwards, Bentley was included in the squad of twenty-one to travel to the World Cup. He was selected ahead of Jackie Milburn for the 2-0 win over Chile, but next came the infamous 0-1 defeat at the hands of the United States. Bentley missed a sitter in that game and was switched to play out wide for the second half. Further changes followed and for England's third and final game of the tournament – a 0-1 defeat by Spain – Milburn was recalled in Bentley's place.

Although he never became an England regular, Bentley's eye-catching mobility saw him given a roving commission by Chelsea. He would often drop back to help in midfield and defence, thereby confusing the defenders under orders to mark him at all costs. Don Revie at Manchester City would take these tactics a stage further by becoming a permanently deep-lying centre-forward. Bentley's role as Chelsea skipper meant it was useful for him to be buzzing around all areas of the pitch anyway. He loved being captain and learned much by studying Manchester United's Johnny Carey. Bentley says he himself hardly ever swore on the pitch, something Bentley learned from his father, who insisted that players who swore were poor communicators, unable to express themselves properly.

Bentley was an intelligent footballer and recalled fondly his long chats on the way to training about the finer points of the game with teammate Ron Greenwood. Bentley would catch a train from Park Royal station, near his West London home, meet Greenwood at Greenford, and they would talk football all the way into Fulham Broadway (the new name given to Walham Green Underground station in 1952).

After their initial doubts subsided, Chelsea supporters warmed to Bentley and fifty years later he is widely seen as probably the most influential player in the club's history. He says he got on well with the fans and loved the atmosphere, marvelling at how the applause would spread right round the bowl-shaped terracing and up to the Shed at the back: 'This really did make you glow.'

Winning twelve full England caps and hitting nine England goals – including a hat-trick against Wales – helped make Roy Bentley a big name in English football at that time. He was one of the nation's most feared centre-forwards for the better part of ten years. Like other well-known target-men of the era, he was physically strong and put himself about when he wanted to, but he also had considerable skill and pace, allied to excellent heading ability. A high proportion of his goals came when the pitches were at their heaviest between November and February. The mid-winter 'mud and guts' of English football held no fears for Bentley.

The other senior player to command extra respect from Chelsea teammates around this time was Glasgow-born defender John Harris. Said to be a religious man who carried a bible around with him, Harris was a hard, uncompromising figure on the pitch but a decent guy off it. He developed some intense rivalries with one or two opponents, particularly Jack Rowley of Manchester United. Harris was nearly thirty when he made his Chelsea League debut, but at that point only had twenty-eight official League games to his name, due to the intervention of the War. He had captained the side after signing on loan from Wolves during the War and was signed permanently as soon as the conflict ended. He went on to amass more than 300 League games in ten years.

Around the time of Ted Drake's arrival, Harris was made a lucrative offer by a Midlands club that would have made him England's best paid non-league manager. Perhaps encouraged by Drake's arrival, Harris eventually turned down the £1,000-plus annual salary, plus house and bonus, and stayed put.

The son of a former Newcastle forward, Harris was a teetotal, non-smoking, quiet bachelor who rarely swore and earned himself the soubriquet 'Gentleman John'. Soccer historian Albert Sewell reckons Harris's finest game was against Sunderland in 1950, when he marked danger-man Trevor Ford out of the game. Sunderland had only recently 'stolen' Ford from under Chelsea's nose when he left Aston Villa, and the disappointed Chelsea fans gave Ford a hostile reception. John Harris made it a personal challenge to keep Ford in his pocket that day.

Harris is remembered with deep affection by supporters of the time. Bournemouth-based Alan Scoltock, for example, said: 'Harris was Mister Perfect, very polished and a very trustworthy player.' Harris's tackling and positional sense overcame his lack of pace and he would ultimately be used at full-back as well as centre-half. Drake purchased Stan Wicks in early 1954 to step into Harris's shoes, but Wicks eventually forced his way into the team at the expense of Ron Greenwood, with Harris remaining a key man beyond the age of thirty-eight. Harris's commitment to the Chelsea cause was a fine example to others, and exactly what Ted Drake needed as the important 1954-55 season loomed.

The 1953-54 campaign ended on an anticlimactic note, with Chelsea missing a top-six finish by failing to win any of their last four games. Undaunted, Drake led his men on a globetrotting end-of-season tour which encompassed friendlies in Dublin, Luxembourg, and then seven games in the USA and Canada. While the squad was over in North America, sporting history was made when Roger Bannister broke the four-minute mile in Oxford. And, even nearer to home, Chelsea wing-half Ken Armstrong sat kicking his heels, patiently waiting to see if he would be required for England World Cup duty. Armstrong was one of five men put on 'stand by' for the tournament in Switzerland but, as it turned out, would not be called upon.

Chapter 3

THE LULL BEFORE THE STORM

(August-September 1954)

Lulls often precede a storm, and the summer of 1954 was noticeably quiet at Stamford Bridge. Manager Ted Drake seemed content to start the new season with the same team that had finished the previous term in eighth place.

That side had enjoyed an excellent second half to 1953-54, although their copybook was blotted somewhat by a couple of home defeats near the end. Drake's only activity in the summer 1954 transfer market was to offload pay-rebels Jack Saunders and Bobby Campbell (they both turned down offers of £7 per week), who were in any case past their prime. He also signed Bishop Auckland forward Seamus O'Connell on amateur terms. Drake reckoned that, with a little luck, his squad was now ready to become genuine contenders for the League title. It was an optimistic view, apparently not shared by the press or the majority of supporters.

The big kick-off in August would mark fifty years since this club first kicked a ball in anger. This milestone was noted on the front cover of the impressive sixteen-page match programme, bereft of advertisements in those days, issued for home games in 1954-55. Press pundits felt that if Chelsea's first trophy in fifty years was imminent, it might take the form of the FA Cup. They brushed aside Drake's insistence that his ambitions lay with the League championship. Skipper Roy Bentley had heard it all before, but he told the man from *The People*: 'Wondering how near to the bottom we will finish is old stuff. Nowadays all we think of is how near the top we will be.'

The 1954 close season lasted little more than a month for most Chelsea players, for they did not return from North America until well into June. That tour, playing alongside a team from Glasgow Rangers, was a real eye-opener for the less well-travelled members of the squad. Prior to a game with an American All-Stars team in New Jersey, Chelsea chairman Joe Mears and his ex-showgirl wife were invited by friends to bring the players to a show as part of the promotional build-up to their next match. Twenty minutes after the curtain went up, the chairman decided that the nudity on stage was not suitable for young, impressionable footballers and they were led grumpily out of the theatre.

The protracted tour had involved ten games in thirty-seven days, coming immediately after a 52-match English campaign (including friendlies), so the subsequent summer rest was well-earned. Reporting back for pre-season training in July, the players were faced with the urgent figure of Ted Drake and the calmer, more measured approach of trainer Jack Oxberry as they encountered their first job of the new campaign – to climb onto the weighing scales. Inevitably, several players were found to have have added a few pounds too many.

Goalkeeper Chick Thomson recalled that the squad would be divided by Drake and Oxberry into three groups, depending on the weight they had put on. The naturally slim players, who didn't grow flabby no matter how much they ate, were put in one group. Those who were a pound or two over their fighting weight would go in the middle group, and the real heavyweights with a serious problem would be in the third section. This last section included Thomson's fellow goalkeeper Bill Robertson, and Bobby Smith, a robust reserve centre-forward. Smith's tendency to rotundity was frustrating for Drake and was one of several reasons the pair did not always see eye to eye. Thomson recalls poor Smith being made to run around in a plastic suit with woolly jumpers on top, secured with plastic, to make him shed bucketloads of sweat.

Drake seemed to have little faith in Smith these days, for the player had faded from the first team scene after two highly promising seasons at the start of his career. Rescued from his job in the coalmines near Redcar, Smith had debuted at just seventeen in 1950 and his first two years in a blue shirt saw him bludgeon twenty-five goals in sixty games. After Drake's arrival at Stamford Bridge, however, Smith's career stalled and he only mustered one goal in fifteen appearances over the subsequent two years. To outsiders, this was a real mystery, but Smith later revealed that he felt cold-shouldered by Drake following a training incident in which Ken Armstrong's arm was broken. Although Bentley, and Armstrong himself, assured the manager the damage was accidental, Smith reckons he was 'out in the cold' from that moment on.

Drake often preferred to use Les Stubbs or Seamus O'Connell instead of Smith, even though the big man's up-and-at-'em style was unsettling for opposing defences and made him look a good partner for the quicker and more mobile Bentley. Smith told author David Lane: 'After I'd got to know him, I thought Ted Drake was a horrible man. Ted make it clear he didn't like me and I never really got a chance at Chelsea with him as manager.' Despite goals galore in Chelsea reserves, it came as no surprise when Smith was eventually off-loaded to Tottenham. It was at White Hart Lane that his career would take off in spectacular fashion and he became a key member of the Tottenham double winning side of 1962, and earned thirteen England caps.

This clash of personalities meant Drake failed to extract the best from a highly regarded, if idiosyncratic player, a rare blemish on the record of a manager who had recruited so many footballers from the lower divisions and successfully moulded them into top-flight stars.

As the FA did not permit public friendlies between League teams during the close season, most clubs staged public 'trial' matches, billed as 'Probables v Possibles, or Reds v Blues, or such-like. This served to bring in a little revenue at the gate, and gave the players match practice before the League curtain went up. In the summer of 1954 Brentford landed themselves in hot water by staging a pre-season game with Leyton Orient. Although ostensibly a private game, someone from the FA thought differently, and is said to have telephoned Griffin Park while the game was in progress. A message was relayed to Bees manager Bill Dodgin, whereupon he marched onto the pitch and ordered everybody off. A Brentford spokesman claimed they had done nothing wrong as it was strictly a training game behind closed doors, and the only public who saw any action were a handful of small boys who had climbed over a gate. The FA was not impressed.

The new season of 1954-55 began with mixed fortunes for Chelsea at Leicester, newly promoted after fifteen years outside the top flight. The lively Foxes missed many chances before Mal Griffiths netted, but a one-goal advantage was not enough to prevent a late Chelsea breakaway in which Bentley forced an equaliser. The result, 1-1, was a real let-off, and it might have been worse for City when Johnny McNichol went close to pinching both points, but wasted a golden chance in the dying seconds. Sadly, for Chelsea, lively winger Frank Blunstone picked up an ankle injury that would keep him out for nearly three months – just at a time when his name was being aired as an England prospect. In addition to bemoaning Blunstone's ill-fortune, Drake was scathing about the Filbert Street grass, which he felt had been allowed to grow too long. Still, one observer who was impressed by Chelsea on this opening day was John Camkin of the *News Chronicle*: 'I liked Chelsea. I liked the delicate sharp thrusts which often left Bentley and Stubbs clear of the full-backs.'

Blunstone's No 11 shirt was handed to the taller, but equally pacy figure of Jim Lewis, who Drake had recruited from Walthamstow Avenue on amateur forms. With the maximum wage still governing footballers' pay-packets, Lewis knew he could earn more as a travelling salesman and remained an amateur even though his early Chelsea career featured some memorable goalscoring appearances. His full-time job took him all round the country, and he had informal arrangements with various clubs whereby he could just turn up and train whenever he happened to be in that area. At Walthamstow, Lewis had starred in their 1952 FA Amateur Cup winning team, when his teammates included Essex and England cricketer Trevor Bailey. When turning out for the East London side, and the England amateur representative team, Lewis was usually employed as a rampaging centre-forward, but Drake liked to use him out wide and he proved a capable deputy for little Blunstone.

Forty-eight hours after the draw at Leicester, Frank Hill's Burnley came to Stamford Bridge for a Monday afternoon game. The season's opening home fixture proved – for an hour at least – to be a drab affair. The mediocre first half sparked bouts of slow-handclapping among the below-average crowd (an activity described as a 'new fashion' at football matches), but just as a goalless draw was looking likely, stand-in Lewis created the winning goal. Fellow winger Eric Parsons put away Lewis's cross, whereafter Chelsea hung on to their lead for dear life. They even survived a last-kick scare when Bill Holden thundered a drive against Robertson's crossbar.

So far, so good – three points from two games when they could easily have earned only one. The players and supporters were in good heart for the visit of Bolton the following Saturday, and nearly 53,000 turned out to see Lewis steal the show again. It was a topsy-turvy encounter, typical of unpredictable Chelsea, with Wanderers surging into a two-goal lead within twenty minutes. Lewis's cross just before the interval saw Bentley pull a goal back, and Chelsea came out after the break in fighting mood. Lewis equalised after his first attempt hit a post and then, with less than fifteen minutes to go, a swirling corner by the ubiquitous Lewis was headed into his own net by the unfortunate full-back John Ball to clinch another dramatic victory.

Chelsea had the rare chance to go top of the League when they visited Turf Moor, Burnley, three days later. They came agonisingly close to the victory that would have taken them there. In sweltering heat, Bentley broke a goalless deadlock by lobbing a neat goal over the head of keeper Colin McDonald with fifteen minutes left, but victory was snatched away with eighty-eight minutes on the clock. A scramble led to a scruffy Burnley equaliser, with Chelsea arguing furiously that Bill Holden and scorer Brian Pilkington had illegally buffeted Robertson, but the pleas fell on deaf ears. The single point earned was, however, enough to put the Blues second in the table.

Big Robertson was not happy about the treatment he had received at Turf Moor. He cut a hefty figure and could usually hold his own when things got physical in the six-yard box (which, in the 1950s was often), but he felt aggrieved at the lack of protection from the referee on this occasion. Born in the Home Counties, Robertson had joined Chelsea after serving with the RAF and replaced Harry Medhurst in the first team near the end of 1950-51, when Chelsea had been threatened by relegation. Known for being a nervous wreck before kick-off, Robertson apparently needed a couple of stiff whiskies before his debut at home to Liverpool. This must have done the trick, for he kept a clean sheet and also appeared in the final three games of that campaign, playing a vital role as relegation was narrowly avoided.

By the time Drake arrived at the club in 1952, Robertson was the established goalkeeper, but the new boss signed Charlie 'Chick' Thomson from Clyde, presumably to give Robertson serious competition. Over the next few seasons, Robertson was generally first choice, but by no means an automatic name on the team-sheet. He was a good shot-stopper, possessing famously huge hands, but his teammates love to recall the stage-fright he suffered before every game. It is said he used to quietly pace the dressing room floor, chain-smoking, and would reluctantly take the field, shaking like a leaf. Once the game got going, however, he was solid as a rock and highly reliable.

A rare error that Robertson was never allowed to forget came in an away game in the north, when he threw the ball out, intending to find the feet of Ken Armstrong. He misjudged his aim, though, and the opposition made the most of the blunder, leaving Drake speechless. He forbade Robertson, and his deputy Thomson, from ever throwing the ball out again, telling them to stick to drop-kicks. Unfortunately for Thomson, in training a few days later he forgot this instruction and threw the ball out, sparking a huge row.

Thomson followed a family tradition in becoming a goalkeeper, for his father had enjoyed a career of more than twenty years in the professional game, mostly with Brighton. Thomson Junior had several years with Clyde before a bust-up with the club's chairman led to him being shown the door. Ted Drake, who had first watched Thomson while managing Reading, quickly snapped him up. Thomson did a good job when called upon, but was never one of the most fashionable of footballers. In contrast to Robertson, Thomson was a lanky individual whose kit looked baggy and unkempt. He was known for his liking for string gloves, held together by an elastic band, and an ancient flat cap, of which he was particularly fond, but which would prompt cat-calls from opposition fans.

Cardiff City came to Stamford Bridge at the beginning of September 1954 with Chelsea again knowing that victory might well put them top of the table. But, just as at Burnley five days earlier, the contest ended disappointingly in a draw, with both goals coming in the latter stages. Robertson was at fault when Mike Tiddy's hopeful shot from outside the area sailed in after seventy-five minutes. Fortunately for the red-faced keeper, Lewis was on-song again, and six minutes from time popped up to head home an Armstrong cross. The unbeaten start thus remained intact, but Chelsea knew they faced a tough test the following Monday when the legendary Tom Finney brought his Preston North End side to the Bridge.

Finney was an astonishingly skilful winger, regarded at the time – and since – as possibly the best ever. Many even put him ahead of Stanley Matthews because of his much higher scoring rate. By now, Finney was thirty-two and entering a period in his career when injuries began to take their toll. Back trouble was plaguing him due to a damaged sciatic nerve, and knee and shoulder problems would follow. Nevertheless his legendary toughness saw him overcome these handicaps. He would ultimately surprise many observers by playing on until 1960, sometimes in a withdrawn centre-forward role.

This particular visit to Chelsea saw Finney still coming to terms with the nightmare FA Cup final a few months earlier. Much had been expected of him when Preston reached the 1954 final to face West Brom, but Finney had a rare off-day and was played out of the game by opposing captain Len Millard – West Brom taking the Cup 3-2. It was probably Finney's saddest hour and the press gleefully screamed the next day that he had failed to live up to the achievements of Matthews in the famous Wembley final the previous year.

Nevertheless, football fans everywhere held Finney in the highest esteem and the regulars at Stamford Bridge were no exception. Blues fullback Stan Willemse would remark later that he was amazed to hear the Chelsea fans cheering whenever Finney got past him. Finney's sublime skills inspired that sort of reaction. He was the gentleman footballer of the 1950s: never booked, sent off or even ticked-off by referees. Later he would be made an OBE, become President of his club, a magistrate and chairman of his local health authority, while continuing to run his own plumbing business. And in the 1998 New Year Honours list he would received the ultimate accolade – a knighthood.

Finney was far tougher than his slight frame suggested and early in his life overcame health problems. At the age of six, he suffered an infected gland in his neck which meant twice-weekly hospital visits for many years until the gland was removed. He hoped to be a footballer but his father Alf insisted he learned a trade. So he became an apprentice plumber – an occupation he was to pursue all his life, even at the height of his international fame. Finney always stayed loyal to his beloved Preston, even when Italian club Palermo tried to tempt him with a £10,000 signing on fee, £130 a month in wages, bonuses of up to £100 a game, a Mediterranean villa, a luxury car and free travel to and from Italy for his family. They also offered Preston a £30,000 transfer fee. In the 1950s this was fantasy-land, but down-to-earth Finney turned it down.

Finney preferred to stay in England and do battle with the likes of Stan Willemse, who – legend has it – was the only player ever to provoke an aggressive retaliation out of Tom Finney. A long-standing Preston supporter, who also spent many years serving on the local magistrates bench alongside him, told the *Daily Telegraph*: 'In all his time at Deepdale, I only once saw him get angry. A Chelsea full-back called Stan Willemse didn't just kick Tom up in the air, but kicked him on the way down. When Tom got up he drew his fist back. But nothing more.'

Willemse himself clearly remembered this September 1954 meeting with Preston: 'In this game Finney was making a monkey out of me and the Chelsea fans were cheering him! They would obviously prefer Chelsea to win but the home fans in those days would often clap and cheer if the opposition scored a good goal or there was an individual piece of skill from the other side.'

The game was an entertaining top-of-the-table clash and after Chelsea dominated the first half with no reward, Finney sent the ball low across the Chelsea box and Bobby Foster side-footed it past Robertson. Chelsea failed to find a way back over the remaining twenty minutes and Preston scaled the top of the League, to the delight of new manager Frank Hill, who had only been in the job a matter of weeks.

The two sides met again nine days later in the Deepdale return, and this time the tables were turned. With Willemse doing his level best to subdue Finney, the Blues roared into a two-goal lead though McNichol and Parsons. Inevitably, the home side fought hard in the final stages, particularly after Charlie Wayman pulled a goal back. The nearest they came to an equaliser came from efforts by hobbling wing-half Willie Forbes, who had been injured and was supposed to be a mere 'passenger' on the left wing. The result delighted Drake, coming as it did hot on the heels of a 1-1 draw at Manchester City when Chelsea had been a mite fortunate to come away with a point.

Encouraged by these early results, especially the solid away displays, a crowd just short of 60,000 packed into Stamford Bridge the following week for the visit of Everton. But, in time honoured fashion, Chelsea fluffed their lines. The Merseysiders escaped with a 2-0 win, punishing the home side for missing some inviting chances early in the proceedings. Two fine away results had been followed by a disappointing home defeat – just the sort of sequence that infuriated Stamford Bridge regulars before and since.

John Major – Prime Minister, 1990-97 – summed up the feeling in his autobiography: 'I have spent many a happy afternoon at Stamford Bridge and many frustrating ones as well, as Chelsea demonstrate their legendary unpredictability. Supporting Chelsea over the years has been a roller-coaster ride, but it has been a great aid in developing a philosophical view.'

And the former Right Honourable Member for Huntingdon is, inevitably, not the only Chelsea fan to have examined the club's inconsistency from a philosophical point of view. Brian Barnard, who also started watching Chelsea in the mid-1950s, told the club's official website recently: 'In your heart of hearts you know [the highs] aren't real and can't last and … you dare not trust [them]. The lows of disappointment are mixed with anger at yourself for allowing your hopes to be raised so that they could be betrayed by another futile incompetent performance – all the time you loathe yourself for letting it happen again and again, and promise yourself that nothing Chelsea could do in future would ever bring you again to that state.'

Chelsea had a quick opportunity to get the Everton defeat out of their systems. The visit to lowly Sheffield United was scheduled for forty-eight hours later, yet another Monday game unlikely to pull in a big crowd because of its afternoon kick-off. Bentley lost the toss, Chelsea kicked towards a bright sun, but after ninety seconds Lewis swooped to score after Parsons' effort was blocked and the ball ran free. The Blades hit back and deserved their first-half equaliser through Graham Shaw. They exerted more heavy pressure after the interval, but somehow Chelsea survived and broke Yorkshire hearts by pinching a winner ten minutes from time. Bentley's low centre from the left found Stubbs, who dived bravely to head home. It was Stubbs' first goal in eighteen League games, but his joy was short-lived. Stubbs injured his thigh in the act of scoring and would be absent from the next game.

The win at Bramall Lane saw Chelsea climb back into the top six – despite their two home defeats from the ten matches thus far. Chelsea's other teams were also faring well as the summer leaves began to turn brown. The reserves were going well, trouncing Arsenal 4-1 and hitting eighteen goals in four games, and the goal-glut spread to the 'A' team. On 23rd September the third string hammered Dunstable 11-3 to go top of the Metropolitan League. They were 7-0 up by half-time, and six of the goals came from Miles Spector in the No 11 shirt. Spector had recently completed his college research studies, allowing him to resume a football career that had been interrupted in 1952-53, just after he made a dramatic bow in the first team.

The undoubted highlight of the opening two months of the season came at St James' Park, Newcastle, at the end of September. Chelsea chalked up only the club's second-ever win at Newcastle – the first was back in 1909 – and Bobby Smith took the eye, deputising for the injured Stubbs. By a quirk of fate, all three Chelsea goals came from ex-Newcastle players, all netted in a whirlwind opening twenty minutes. The first was a shot from Bentley from out on the flank, which flew past the diving Ronnie Simpson, the second from the boot of McNichol, and the third a fierce left-footer from Bentley.

For a spell, the Geordies' rugged skipper Jimmy Scoular went in goal, to allow the injured Simpson to receive treatment, a situation which must have gladdened Chelsea hearts. Scoular had a reputation as a hard-man and his removal into goal will have saved the visiting forwards at least a few bruises. Winger Blunstone reflected later: 'Scoular was a dirty so-and-so. I remember kicking him by accident [in another match] and him telling me he'd get me later. Derek Saunders was about to take a throw and I was shaking my head to say don't give it to me because Scoular was behind and I could sense it was payback time. He threw it straight to my feet, though, and I was immediately kicked up in the air and the trainer had to come on. Scoular asked me if I now wanted to call it quits and I accepted!'

Shortly before the game at St James' Park, Ted Drake had turned up at a Newcastle cinema to present prizes for a cartoon competition, making this guest appearance alongside Ben Warriss, a nationally-known comedian. Warriss chatted with Drake about football and ended up attending the match. Drake was fulsome in praise of his team's victory, unhesitatingly calling it the best performance of the season thus far, with the team doing 'brilliantly'. He highlighted the side's resilience in the away games at Sheffield and Newcastle, when intense home pressure had been thwarted. On both occasions Chelsea had lost the toss and had to kick towards a bright sun in the first period.

Winger Lewis, recalling the Newcastle game, said Drake had instructed veteran defender John Harris before kick-off not to allow left-winger Bobby Mitchell get past him more than twice – and if he did, he was to kick him up in the air and make sure it didn't happen a third time. Poor Mitchell was sent sprawling after about ten minutes, said Lewis, and was rarely seen for the remainder of the game.

Ted Drake was a busy man over the final few days of September 1954. He had been invited to take charge of a London Football Association representative side, but was also keeping tabs on the situation at Second Division Leeds, where brilliant young Welsh international John Charles was said to be unsettled and ready for a move. Here was an outstanding player that most First Division managers would have loved to sign, and Drake made no secret of the fact that he would relish the chance to bring Charles to Stamford Bridge.

On the day that twenty-three-year-old 'Big John' had his formal transfer request considered by the Elland Road directors, Drake was – frustratingly, perhaps – out of the country, supervising the London FA side over in Hanover. Although Chelsea's Jim Lewis had to withdraw, due to an ankle injury sustained at Newcastle, the London FA party still included seven men from Stamford Bridge – Drake (manager), Jack Oxberry (trainer), plus players Willemse, Armstrong, Greenwood, Bentley and Saunders. Despite torrential rain, the game drew a crowd of 40,000 to Hanover Stadium. It was the first match there since major rebuilding work had been completed. Facing a side selected from Lower Saxony clubs, the London boys won 3-1, with Chelsea's Bentley setting up the opener for Jimmy Logie of Arsenal. Chelsea's Armstrong drove home for the second goal and Bentley sewed things up after being sent clear in the second half. Back in England on the same evening, FA Cup holders West Brom and reigning champions Wolves drew 4-4 when contesting the FA Charity Shield under the Molineux floodlights.

One of Drake's first tasks after returning from West Germany was to check on the John Charles situation. The player's transfer request had been sparked by Leeds' poor run, during which he had been switched against his wishes from centre-forward to centre-half. Charles was such an influential player that when the Leeds directors called an emergency meeting to discuss his future, chairman Eric Stanger described their task as 'the most difficult in the 35 years of the club's history'.

In a statement, Stanger painted a clear picture of the situation professional footballers in England faced at that time: 'According to Football League law, John Charles cannot substantially earn any more money with Arsenal, Cardiff City or (if they will forgive me for using them as an illustration) Halifax Town than with Leeds United. He can be paid no more than the legal maximum of £15 a week during the playing season, plus a bonus of £2 for a win and £1 for a draw. A player of his standing can command the customary maximum Football League benefit of £750 every five years, no matter where he plays. Why then does Charles seek a move? As he would be the first to admit, he has been as well treated at

Elland Road as anywhere. He wants to play in First Division football. Can one blame him for that? His abilities are extraordinary and one can scarcely quarrel with any artist for wishing to exploit his talents in the best medium. In Charles' case, he feels it lies in top class football with a better team than Leeds United.'

Reportedly, Chelsea, Cardiff and Arsenal were all ready with substantial bids for Charles, but this hungry trio were foiled when the news was announced on 30th September that Leeds had turned down Charles' transfer request. He was quoted: 'I'm still anxious to play First Division football but what can I do? I was called into the meeting and told that the club would not let me go. I was not really surprised.' It was a dignified response and, to his credit, Charles rolled his sleeves up and continued at centre-half for the good of his club and put his personal ambitions to one side. He would later move to Juventus, but in the meantime, his staying put left Ted Drake a disappointed man. Drake had a side at Stamford Bridge which he believed was already capable of challenging for the First Division title, but being able to spend Joe Mears' money on a player like John Charles would have been a major step forward.

Chapter 4

FALLING OFF THE PACE

(October-November 1954)

Stamford Bridge was bursting at the seams for the first match of October 1954, with a lock-out crowd of more than 67,000 greeting the visit of FA Cup holders and current League leaders West Bromwich Albion. After notching up three successive away wins in September, here was fourth-placed Chelsea's chance to show their true worth. In his programme notes, Ted Drake called for extra vocal encouragement to end the poor run of home form and blamed 'trying too hard' for the player's recent flops at Stamford Bridge.

There were certainly no signs of stage-fright against West Brom as Roy Bentley netted his 100th League goal for the club in the early stages, but the supporters' delight was stifled within minutes when Ronnie Allen bagged a soft equaliser. Goals by Jim Lewis and Eric Parsons after the break put Chelsea in the driving seat, but Albion hit back in the final minutes. After winger George Lee had pegged one goal back, their wily captain and left-back Len Millard – who had been enduring a nightmare match against nippy Parsons – strode upfield to fire a tremendous equaliser past Bill Robertson. So Albion stayed top and Chelsea remained fourth.

That six-goal thriller provided most of the streamer headlines in the press the next day, but there was mention further down the pages of an unusual occurrence at the game between Aldershot and Watford in Division Three (South). It was reported that Shots defender Charlie Billington had been pulled up by referee Bill Ling for making a 'hissing noise' just as Watford's Roy Brown was about a to shoot. Mr Ling gave Billington a ticking off and Watford were awarded an indirect free-kick for ungentlemanly conduct!

Failure to beat West Brom after being two goals ahead seemed to knock the stuffing out of the Blues over the next few weeks. A string of poor results followed. Not even some target practice against Division Three (South) Brentford in a friendly helped dispel the gloom. Chelsea beat the Bees 4-0 in a Tuesday night game arranged to officially open the Griffin Park floodlights. Drake gave a first run-out that night to the amateur forward Seamus O'Connell and certainly liked what he saw.

O'Connell was the son of a wealthy cattle dealer and did not wish to become a full-time footballer. When called upon by Chelsea, he would commute to London from Carlisle – 'often being spotted on the train carrying his boots, tied by the laces, round his neck' – according to historian Albert Sewell. O'Connell was happy to stay on the books of crack non-league outfit Bishop Auckland and play for Chelsea on an occasional basis. It seems a strange choice in today's world of huge football salaries, but in the days of the maximum wage, a man with a reasonable income outside the game would need to remain amateur to maintain his standard of living.

John Burton, who later became Tony Blair's constituency agent, was a fellow amateur player at Bishop Auckland, alongside O'Connell. In Burton's autobiography *Grit in the Oyster*, the Northern non-league scene of the 1950s is exposed, with revelations that players were paid generous expenses despite their amateur status. As for Seamus O'Connell, 'he couldn't even afford to play for Chelsea because he was getting more at Bishop Auckland,' reflected Burton.

Born of Irish parents, O'Connell became something of an enigma to both colleague and supporters. Working in the cattle trade in Cumberland meant he didn't train with Chelsea and only showed up for a few hours on match-days. Subsequently, after his short career with Chelsea ended, it seems he did another vanishing act as far as football historians are concerned – but more of that later. In the meantime, Drake felt O'Connell could do a job in the First Division and after watching him play well in another friendly, this time at Hull City, made plans to give him his debut in the League side in place of Les Stubbs, whose recent goal return had been poor.

Chelsea slumped to a single-goal defeat at Huddersfield on 9th October and slipped down to ninth in the table. High-flying Manchester United were next up and, for their visit to Stamford Bridge, Drake took the plunge and sent a message to Carlisle, requesting Seamus O'Connell to bring his boots to London to face Matt Busby's mighty team. Just under 56,000 turned out for the game, a figure that would have been higher had the local buses not been affected by strike action. Those spectators who walked or cycled to the game were in for the football treat of their lives. It was a contest that Ted Drake would later describe thus: 'It was the match of a lifetime and nothing quite as remarkable has ever been seen here at Stamford Bridge.'

He was not exaggerating. Even *The Times*' correspondent was moved to describe the match as 'sweeping aside almost all the cobwebs of English football with a giant broom'. The game was a spectacular ninety minutes packed with eleven goals and relentless attacking football. The young giant Duncan Edwards set up Dennis Viollet for a fifteenth-minute opening goal, but five minutes later Bentley provided the pass from which O'Connell swept in an equaliser. On the half-hour Bentley crossed for Lewis to convert from close range. United bounced back immediately and Tommy Taylor levelled, with Viollet forcing them ahead again shortly before the interval.

At the start of the second period, poor defending by Stan Willemse allowed Taylor to make it 4-2 to United. A neat flick by Johnny Berry left Ron Greenwood floundering and Viollet completed his hat-trick, this being United's fourth goal in a nineteen-minute purple passage. Although Chelsea were down, they were certainly not out. They brought the score back to 3-5 when Ken Armstrong headed in Parsons' corner, but irre-pressible United restored their three-goal advantage when Jackie Blanchflower deflected a shot past Robertson. Still Chelsea wouldn't lie down. Four minutes later, O'Connell steamed onto Armstrong's through ball to crack home a beauty. Then, amazingly, they were just a single goal behind after O'Connell completed a debut hat-trick, knocking in the rebound after Parsons headed a Bentley cross against the woodwork. The ground was by now a cauldron, the disbelieving crowd at fever pitch. Eleven goals, Chelsea 5-6 down but very much in the ascendancy, and there were still fourteen minutes of play left.

The Blues poured forward, forcing United to back-pedal desperately in the closing stages. Given what had gone before, it was astonishing that there was no further scoring. Wing-half Derek Saunders admitted later it was a bad day for defenders and confessed that he and Willemse were responsible for at least a couple of the goals through slack marking at corners: 'But it was a lovely game to be involved in and it was an amaz-ing finale.'

Speaking some fifty years later, Roy Bentley admitted he could not remember a match like it, and said: 'If it had gone on a few more min-utes we'd have gone on to win, no question.' He added: 'Mind you, eleven was not the most goals in a game I played in, for I remember a match for Newcastle when Len Shackleton scored six as we beat Newport 13-0.' Ted Drake swallowed his disappointment at the outcome and declared that football had been the winner, and he was full of praise for hat-trick man O'Connell, who had experienced a dream debut, despite the final scoreline.

The spectators had been treated to an unforgettable feast and one in particular was delighted with his afternoon's entertainment – especially as he had never expected to be at Stamford Bridge in the first place.

Northerner Eddie Roberts was on leave from his National Service duties and had come to London intending to see the big clash between English middle-distance runner Chris Chataway and the Russian, Vladimir Kutz. Finding the gates locked at White City, with a capacity crowd inside, Norman had to change his plans. He studied the week's sporting fixtures and plumped for football at Chelsea instead: 'Once we got through the turnstiles, everyone started running for the paddock, where you had to pay again,' recalled Eddie, who no doubt concluded that the double admission charge had ended up good value for money.

Stamford Bridge had witnessed some marvellous sporting moments, but nothing quite like this game. The cavernous stadium, with its vast banks of open terracing, was one of the biggest grounds in the country at the time, capable of holding crowds of 75,000. The open nature of the stadium, and the fact that the greyhound track separated the fans from the field of play, tended to dilute the noise levels somewhat and deaden the atmosphere, but regular Chelsea-goers from those days nevertheless have happy memories of their Saturday afternoon meeting place. Tony Banks MP was just one of thousands who returned week after week, undaunted by the hardships of poor facilities and being at the mercy of the winter elements. He recalls:

'The ground was huge and had enormous open terracing. There were large areas of uncovered space, plus the East Stand and a rickety little stand on stilts to the right of it, which looked rather dangerous actually. The rest was open to the rain and elements. Vast numbers stood on the terraces and there was a good atmosphere, although not intimidating to the players as at some grounds, because the crowds were a long way back from the pitch. You would have to get there quite early to get a favourite place and us kids would work our way through to the spot we wanted.

'Chelsea would get huge crowds in those days and there would be great surges forward and back again, but you'd always find yourself back at the spot you started from. It didn't seem dangerous, for everyone was sensible and good natured and going to football didn't seem a hazardous pursuit at all. There would be a big crush getting out, too, and for a laugh us kids would often play around by jumping in the air in order to get wedged between the human tide of adults as it swept along. We would then find ourselves moving along without our feet on the ground – that would be a great laugh.'

Another boyhood fan, Alan Scoltock, recalled that the 'real' support-ers – the fully-committed partisans – used to occupy The Shed area, and the bulk of these were local people: 'There were reasonable facilities there for that time, with the dog track often being used in the evenings.

On summer Saturdays when there was no football, the dog racing was very popular with football fans too. For all matches I would always go to stand at the same spot, just outside The Shed. It was open to the elements. There were often very big crowds and many would arrive early. Occasionally the band would play and kids would be passed over the heads to the front to make sure they could see everything.

'Occasionally you'd get a small group or two of away fans. I remember Portsmouth used to bring a big following to Chelsea in those days – I can remember them singing 'Play up Pompey' all the time. My very first game was against Stoke, who had Stanley Matthews in their side, before he moved on to Blackpool. My dad took me at that time. He never got excited like some of the fans. Not many people travelled to away games in those days, for there were no motorways and every journey was difficult, having to negotiate every little town en route. Main roads always went through all the towns, for there were no by-passes.'

Now exiled in the USA, 1950s fan Alec McKay's lasting memory of Stamford Bridge is of a 'dark and spacious' place: 'When I went it was mostly terracing plus the big East Stand, The Shed, and an odd two-storey structure to the left of the stand. I used to stand on the halfway line, halfway up and was usually able to get a place behind a crush barrier for support, since I used to get there quite early.'

Richard Posner can bring his boyhood memories of the Bridge easily to mind: 'The greyhound track surrounding the pitch meant that there was a huge gap between the players and the crowd and ball boys were used to retrieve the ball for throw-ins, corner and goal-kicks. There was only one proper stand, the East, which had covered seating with standing below it. There was The Shed, plus the old North Stand which provided some further covered seating with standing under. What remained, the entire west side of the ground up to the Shed and the North Stand, was completely open uncovered terracing for standing only. People would stand, without any protection from the elements, and watch "The Unpredictables" week in, week out. Also, at any time you looked at the mass of terracing from the comfort of our covered seats, there would always be flares from matches or lighters lighting up cigarettes. At every single second, you could clearly see the flames of a large number of cigarettes being lit.'

Chelsea had an immediate chance to get the Manchester United defeat out of their system with a marathon trip down to play Second Division Plymouth in a Monday night friendly. Drake fielded his full first team and O'Connell bagged another two goals in a 5-1 win. Regrettably, this comfortable workout did not have the effect of boosting League form and a

0-1 defeat at Blackpool five days later dropped Chelsea down to twelfth place in the table, below halfway. That game was played on a treacherous, muddy surface and Chelsea's uncompromising approach did not endear them to the home fans. Parsons picked up a booking and there were mistimed tackles galore, some of them perhaps excusable in the conditions.

The jeering home fans were put in worse humour when their star forward, Allan Brown, picked up the latest in a catalogue of injuries. Poor Brown had missed the 1951 FA Cup final due to a knee problem and then the 1953 final too, after breaking his leg. Ewan Fenton, another player who found himself in the referee's notebook, netted a second-half penalty to decide this mud-spattered, undistinguished encounter. The symmetry of Chelsea's record at this point must have pleased anyone with an eye for statistics: They had earned fifteen points from fifteen games, they had scored twenty-three and conceded twenty-three, and had won five, drawn five and lost five. Balanced perhaps, but these figures were hardly the hallmark of champions.

October ended with a 1-2 home defeat by Charlton Athletic, inflicted by two early goals from South African Eddie Firmani. It was Chelsea's sixth successive game at Stamford Bridge without victory and Drake was forced to make changes to try and halt the slide down the League table. For the trip to Sunderland, cultured centre-half Ron Greenwood was asked to stand down for big Stan Wicks, who had been patiently waiting in the wings since Drake signed him from Reading nine months earlier. Les Stubbs was also recalled, in place of O'Connell.

Earlier that week Drake had rebuffed enquiries from Leyton Orient boss Alec Stock, who was interested in signing either Stubbs or reserve centre-forward Bobby Smith. Drake said neither was for sale. The manager's third change saw Frank Blunstone return in place of Jim Lewis, following Blunstone's long injury absence. Some fans were surprised to see O'Connell left out of the team and also by the fact that Drake had not managed to sign him up on professional terms after his dramatic debut. 'I haven't even asked him,' Drake told the *News of the World*. 'As long as he's happy playing for Chelsea I'm not worried. He's the complete player and fits in the Chelsea plan as things are.'

Despite a bad start at Roker Park, the team changes worked well and Chelsea banished their autumn blues by fighting back to force a 3-3 draw. The home side had cruised into a two-goal lead in the first eighteen minutes, but Johnny McNichol struck twice to even things up, and Stubbs netted a cracking long-range effort to put the Blues ahead. The joy was short-lived as Sunderland levelled within a minute, but overall this match would prove something of a turning point in Chelsea's season. Wicks was not overawed by making his debut in front of 42,000 partisan 'Mackems' and looked composed and resourceful. The omens were not good for Greenwood, though. He was by now almost thirty-three, and although still a skilful and astute performer, he no longer had the speed and sharpness of the younger Wicks. Everyone had assumed that the lanky Wicks would come in to replace the veteran John Harris, but this reliable stalwart was performing as well as ever at full-back and it was Greenwood who got the chop. Greenwood was unhappy to be sidelined and before long sought a transfer, subsequently accepting a move to Second Division neighbours Fulham.

In the run-up to that Sunderland game, a mysterious rumour had circulated in West London that Chelsea full-backs Harris and Willemse had lost their lives in a road accident. This false story spread so quickly that Chelsea asked Fulham to broadcast a statement at their home match with Stoke City on 6th November, reassuring the public that no such tragedy had occurred. The Fulham crowd were informed that the two full-backs were alive and well and playing for the Blues up at Sunderland that very day.

Blunstone's long-awaited return from injury at Sunderland was a boost for the team, and his display earned him a surprise call-up to the England squad for the fixture with Wales at Wembley just four days later. Not only was Blunstone set for his international debut, but manager Walter Winterbottom and the selectors also recalled Roy Bentley to lead the England attack. Bentley already had seven caps to his name, but had been largely left out in the cold since the 1950 World Cup fiasco against he USA. England's recent double humiliation by the Hungarians was still fresh in many minds and it was a mix-and-match side that was selected to to face Wales as part of the rebuilding programme. Surprise choices Blunstone and Bentley were accompanied in attack by the wastefully under-capped maestro Len Shackleton and by forty-year-old winger Stan Matthews. Bill Slater, who might have joined Chelsea had he not been shown the door by office staff two years earlier, made his England debut alongside skipper Billy Wright.

Bentley celebrated his recall by sinking the Welsh with a splendid hat-trick. Two of his goals came from far-post headers after exchanging passes with Matthews, and the hat-trick was completed within a fifteen-minute spell. 'To score three goals in the shadow of the twin towers was quite a privilege,' he recalled. John Charles, leading the Welsh attack with fire and flair, scored twice to bring the scores level at 2-2 before Bentley won the game two minutes from the end of a thrilling match on a rain-saturated Wembley surface. The much-lauded young talent Charles was playing at Wembley for the first time. He very nearly stole the show, but Bentley's late goal ensured it was the Chelsea man who grabbed all the headlines the following morning.

It was naturally an exciting night for Blunstone, who had only recently turned twenty. He was still completing his National Service at this time, but had an arrangement whereby he would be released for Chelsea games. The story goes that he returned to his barracks after Chelsea's match at Sunderland to be told by fellow soldier-footballer Tosh Chamberlain that their commanding officer wanted Blunstone in his office immediately. Chamberlain, a winger with Fulham, was known as a practical joker, and at first Blunstone refused to cooperate, thinking he was being set up. Eventually he went in and was curtly told he'd been picked for England. The officer, without so much as a word of congratulation, barked that he would be allowed to play only if he was back in barracks by the following morning at eight. It emerged later that Ronnie Allen of West Brom had been Winterbottom's first choice, but was unavailable due to injury. Despite Blunstone's lack of match-fitness, Winterbottom decided to take the plunge with the Chelsea winger.

It was a whirlwind few days for the boy from Crewe, and by the time he had reported for England duty on the Monday at the Hendon Hall Hotel in North London, he was feeling unwell. Winterbottom dosed him up with medicine and he played against Wales despite feeling under the weather. Having clubmate Bentley alongside him was of enormous help, for he acted as a sort of father figure and helped calm Blunstone's nerves. With fourteen members of his family up in the stands looking on, Blunstone did well enough on the left flank not to look out of place.

Blunstone had arrived at Chelsea less than two years earlier as a raw eighteen-year-old from his home town club Crewe Alexandra and proved one of Drake's shrewdest signings. He was an exciting little winger, with a penchant for getting his head down and heading for the by-line, where he would whip over crosses for the likes of Bentley. He loved to take his man on and had bags of dribbling skill to add to his obvious pace. An approachable and unassuming young man, one scribe he impressed after arriving in the 'big city' was the legendary Charles Buchan. A leading football writer and former international player, Buchan sang Blunstone's praises after seeing his Chelsea debut at Spurs as a teenager. Chelsea had failed to win their previous four League games, but a reshuffled side containing Blunstone recorded a 3-2 win at White Hart Lane and the young debutant, marked by Alf Ramsey, cracked a second-half equaliser.

Remarkably, this debut had come at the end of a traumatic week, during which Blunstone's brother John was killed in a road accident. Drake phoned the player hours after the funeral with the news that he had been picked to play, but with the option to drop out in view of the family tragedy. After discussions with mum, Blunstone decided his brother would have wanted him to play. He headed back to London, and the rest, as they say, is history.

Recalling those early days in London, Blunstone told one writer: 'I didn't have a clue what I was letting myself in for. Every time I got on the Underground I got lost and I had to go and live in digs after living at home all my life. My signing-on fee for Chelsea was £10, which I got taxed on and my wages were £12 a week. Crewe were happy, though. They had received £8,500 for me in an era when the record transfer was £18,000.' Blunstone admitted he was homesick at first and manager Drake allowed him to have extra days off to return home. Before long he settled into his new life, however, and by the start of 1954-55 had become a key member of Drake's first choice line-up. His return in the November following injury was a big boost for the side.

When old rivals Tottenham visited Stamford Bridge on 13th November, the Chelsea fans gave a huge ovation to their England duo, in recognition of their achievements in midweek against Wales. Bentley said later he had noticed all the noise but had not realised what it was about – the penny finally dropped when he realised the cheers were sparked whenever he received the ball.

After his great start at Sunderland, Wicks did not look quite so happy on his home debut. Bentley recalled noticing Wicks' head drop after he made a hash of a clearance, and the skipper had to nurse him back to full confidence with regular encouragement throughout the game. Chelsea won the match thanks to two early strikes from Bentley and Lewis, and they terminated their run of six games without victory with the luxury of a missed penalty by John Harris.

The defeat saw hapless Spurs sink to twenty-first in the table and they looked in a bad way. Manager Arthur Rowe admitted he was perplexed by their poor run and by the poor form being shown by stalwarts like Alf Ramsey, Eddie Baily, Harry Clarke, Ted Ditchburn and Sonny Walters. They were missing regular full-backs Mel Hopkins and David Dunmore, away on National Service, and Rowe warned that he might have to change Spurs' reputation for never spending big money on new players. Just before the Chelsea defeat he had a substantial bid for Aston Villa's Danny Blanchflower turned down. A week or two later, Villa caved in and Blanchflower was allowed to come to London.

Chelsea headed to Hillsborough to face lowly Sheffield Wednesday on 20th November expecting a fierce scrap, and they were not disappointed, according to Drake. Willemse was injured and finished the game limping along as a makeshift forward, but Chelsea rallied valiantly in the second half and broke away to force a draw with a late equaliser lobbed in by McNichol.

The day before this trip north, Chelsea had announced they would be facing the all-star Hungarian outfit Red Banner (known as Voros Lobogo in their own country) at Stamford Bridge in December. Following the recent exploits of the Hungarian national side, plus the highly-publicised meeting of Wolves and Honved, this new fixture quickly created enormous interest. Chelsea's switchboard was inundated with callers and the game was made all-ticket. Standing tickets were priced at three shillings, and sixpence for the terraces, six shillings and sixpence for the enclosure, and the best seats £1 4s. These were expensive for the 1950s and well above normal Stamford Bridge prices.

December looked like becoming an exciting month, and to prepare for the battles that lay ahead the squad headed for Broadstairs in Kent directly after the Sheffield Wednesday game, to enjoy some invigorating sea air. The week-long break was described in the Chelsea programme as a 'toning-up operation'. Drake explained that the party would be joined later in the week by skipper Bentley, after he had spent a few days training with England. Drake told the press that the break could not come at a better time for his men, but these words came back to haunt him when the English weather decided it didn't want to cooperate with Chelsea that particular week. Soon after the party had arrived at their seaside hotel, stormy weather swept across the country and conditions remained dreadful all week. Off nearby Ramsgate, an 80mph gale tore the South Goodwin lightship from its moorings and the vessel was wrecked, seven men losing their lives.

The bedraggled Chelsea party headed back to London to take on Portsmouth and their change of scene appeared to have worked wonders, for they hammered their highly-placed opposition 4-1. Pompey was a club in mourning at this time, for both trainer Jimmy Nichol and vice-chairman Harry Wain had recently died, and another member of their coaching staff, Jimmy Stewart, was ill in hospital. Sunday school teacher Phil Gunter had recently been earning rave notices for his performances in Pompey's defence, and was being tipped as an England prospect. This wasn't to be Gunter's day, however, and the highlight of the game was an astonishing goal by Les Stubbs, who lashed home a ferocious drive from more than thirty yards to complete the scoring after eighty-five minutes. It would remain clear in Stubbs' memory some fifty years later, for he recalled: 'It was one of my best goals for Chelsea. I was almost 40 yards out, and with the wind behind me and my opponent catching me, I decided to let fly with a ball that weighed almost half a ton. Luck must have been with me that day because it dipped and went in just underneath the bar and Ron Greenwood came running over and said "that's one you will never, ever forget". He was right too! John Harris told the press after the game that it was one of the best goals he'd ever seen.'

So, after a shaky start to the autumn period, Chelsea ended November back in the top half of Division One – albeit only just – and Ted Drake had every reason to think that better times were ahead. The draws at Sunderland and Sheffield Wednesday had been stirring, hard-fought affairs and the home wins over Spurs and Pompey had banished that highly annoying home hoodoo. In addition, star winger Blunstone was fully fit again. Time for a rise up the table?

Chapter 5

THE MARVELS OF MUDDY MOLINEUX
(December 1954)

The lights in the offices of Stamford Bridge in London SW6 burned well into the night during the wet and chilly beginning to December 1954. Club secretary John Battersby could hardly remember such a busy time as this. He and his staff had a mountain of work to plough through. They faced extraordinary demand for tickets for the friendly with Hungarian aces Red Banner and they also had three big League games fast approaching, including a money-spinning Boxing Day clash with Arsenal. In addition, Stamford Bridge had been selected to host an England 'B' game with Italy the following month. Added to which, there was the complication of arrangements for the Red Banner clash to be televised live. To put it mildly, it was a hectic time behind the scenes.

Meanwhile, Chelsea fans had been looking forward to the international at Wembley that saw England take on the world champions, West Germany, on 1st December. The Stamford Bridge faithful were proud of their skipper Roy Bentley's recent match-winning hat-trick against Wales. It was an achievement that had vindicated his recall to the national team – something they had long called for. Walter Winterbottom and the selectors had no choice but to stick with Bentley when the side was named to face the 1954 Jules Rimet Trophy winners at Wembley. West Brom's Ronnie Allen was fit again, however, which meant no place for winger Frank Blunstone, who had made his international debut against Wales. Blunstone was still young and would surely get further chances later on. Although the Germans named a much-changed side from that which had won the World Cup in Switzerland, the occasion was still treated with great anticipation and significance. A full house of 100,000 paid record receipts, most hoping to see England recover some of the pride lost in their recent hammerings by Hungary.

For the England players, some of the tension of the occasion was lifted by the antics of Len Shackleton, the so-called Clown Prince of football. During the pre-kick-off preliminaries, Shackleton left Bentley helpless with mirth. The players had lined up to meet the assembled dignitaries, which included Foreign Secretary Sir Anthony Eden. The players of each side stood facing each other, weighing each other up. Shackleton noticed his counterpart in the German side looking deep in thought, and called out: 'Hey Fritz, if we win the toss today we're going to bat. It might be a bit green, so the ball might move about a bit.' The Germans hadn't a clue what Shackleton was on about, but the joke certainly eased the nerves among his teammates, and Bentley for one was seen to be 'killing himself laughing'.

When the match started, Stanley Matthews rolled back the years to torment the German defenders. His pinpoint cross was headed home by Bentley to give England the lead. Allen doubled the advantage after the interval and the ultimate entertainer Shackleton clinched victory near the end with an impudent chip as the goalkeeper raced out towards him. 'Shack' had thrilled the crowd throughout with his tricks, but was perhaps too much of a maverick for the stiff upper lip selectors. It was his fifth, and last England cap. His non-conformist attitude grated with the men from the FA, but in the eyes of fellow players and fans he was one of the true stars of the era, a man with awesome ability who was criminally under-used by his country.

Bentley came away from Wembley with club matters on his mind. Three days later he was to lead Chelsea out at Molineux, home of the all-conquering League champions Wolves, who had recently boosted their reputation across Europe by hammering the formidable touring side Spartak Moscow. Stan Cullis's boys, back on top of the League, would take on crack Hungarian outfit Honved two days before Chelsea's own tussle with a Magyar side in mid-December. Cullis reckoned his Wolves outfit were currently the best in Europe and held few fears about their ability to overcome mid-table Chelsea on 4th December. He was about to receive a rude awakening.

Although the Molineux pitch was ankle-deep in mud, with the goal-mouth particularly hazardous, the match was a veritable feast. A seven-goal thriller, it was described by *The Times*' correspondent as one of the finest since the War. Chelsea winger Eric Parsons seemed to revel in the mire and went skipping down the flank to cross for Johnny McNichol to open the scoring with a cracking shot. The champions were only momentarily stunned, and levelled within a minute when Peter Broadbent converted a Roy Swinbourne cross. The visitors held firm and refused to crack, unlike the previous season, when they had capsized on this ground by a club record 1-8 scoreline. Shortly after the interval Bentley pounced on a chance to put the Blues ahead again. The lead survived until the 76th minute, when Swinbourne netted Wolves' second equaliser. It was breathless stuff, but the tension intensified further in the closing minutes. Johnny Hancocks converted a penalty with eighty-three minutes on the clock and the points seemed lost for Chelsea. Les Stubbs had other ideas, however, and fired home with four minutes left to bring things level again. Almost straight from the restart Bentley seized on a ball down the middle and broke clear of the Wolves defence to fire past the advancing Bert Williams. The home side could not believe their eyes. Chelsea's players had matched the excitement of the eleven-goal thriller against Manchester United, but even better, this time they had the prize of two points and a shock victory over the League leaders.

If ever a season had a pivotal moment, a true turning point, then this was surely it. Reigning champs Wolves trudged off the swampy pitch with their chins on their chests, unable to comprehend the way they had been robbed of the points in the closing minutes. McNichol recalled later that, coming off the field, one of the home side shook his hand and muttered that Wolves were now going to get 'murdered' by their manager. He was genuinely fearful of disciplinarian Cullis's reaction. Wolves had been in control for most of the game but had let victory slip to a side of inferior ability but greater fighting spirit on the day. Wolves players were about to receive what in modern parlance has become known as 'the hairdryer treatment' from their manger. Centre-forward Dennis Wilshaw later gave an insight into Cullis's management style: he observed that the Wolves team spirit of that time had mainly stemmed from the players' intense hatred of their belligerent manager!

Parsons could claim to be man of the match, despite Wolves' dominance of much of the game. Then thirty-one years old, the winger was enjoying the form of his life. His reputation for being quick-witted and electric-heeled was burgeoning and he had become the scourge of countless full-backs with his scampering bursts of speed. Was he the quickest in the League? Many thought so. Jackie Milburn of Newcastle, Harry Hooper of West Ham, Len Wills of Arsenal, and Billy Bingham of Sunderland were also regarded as fleet of foot, but Doug Wilson of the *News of the World* insisted that if players were to be measured over forty yards instead of 100, then the fastest of all would surely be none other than thirty-nine-year-old Stan Matthews. Although the *News Chronicle* set up technical equipment to prove that Ted Phillips of Ipswich had the most powerful shot in football at this time, it seems nobody felt suitably inspired to find who was the fastest mover.

Victory over Wolves certainly left Chelsea players with aching muscles and a few bruises. Derek Saunders recalled that one of the opposition had clattered into him from behind ('I went down like an ox.'), which led to an ugly scuffle involving Bentley and others. Saunders remembers he only just managed to pull back from giving the guilty man a right hook as the red mist descended and he momentarily lost control: 'The previous year when we'd got hammered 8-1 at Wolves, I'd had a major battle with Bill Slater. There was always a lot of needle in this fixture.'

Saunders was enjoying a good spell in the Chelsea No 6 shirt. This tenacious red-haired wing-half had not missed a game so far this season and his solid defensive work and excellent long-ball distribution was an important ingredient in the team's progress. He first came to Stamford Bridge in 1953, having already made his mark in the England amateur international side and even appeared at the 1952 Olympics. That had been quite a year for Saunders, who had also led his club, Walthamstow Avenue, to victory at Wembley in the FA Amateur Cup. After being offered professional terms by Ted Drake, Saunders quit his job as a shipping clerk. The red-tape involved in getting the paperwork signed delayed his three-week vacation to the Mediterranean, which he had already paid for, but Drake was so keen to get his man that he arranged for Chelsea to cover the costs incurred by the hold-ups – and Derek still got his holiday of a lifetime.

The result at Molineux put Chelsea in good heart for the battles which lay ahead. With the much-anticipated match with Red Banner just four days away, the Hungarian club's squad filed into the Main Stand at Stamford Bridge to watch Chelsea dispose of lowly Aston Villa on 11th December. It was a 4-0 demolition job and Chelsea were never in trouble from the moment a swirling free-kick by Parsons was fumbled into his own net by goalkeeper Keith Jones in the early stages. 'Rabbit' Parsons finished off a long run to create a second for McNichol after the break, and it ended up being a stroll for Chelsea, with two late goals adding the icing to the cake.

Two days later Wolves beat the powerful Honved side under the Molineux floodlights. The win came hot on the heels of their 4-0 destruction of Spartak Moscow and prompted Frank Butler of the *News of the World* to suggest the Midlanders had 'given British soccer a boost in its darkest hour', referring to the national team's double crushing by Hungary in 1953-54. The Honved fixture was Wolves' fourth floodlit friendly against foreign opposition in one season. Earlier they had drawn 0-0 with Vienna and beaten Maccabi Tel Aviv 10-0. Such games were becoming quite the vogue for the bigger clubs. Arsenal played Spartak Moscow twice, going down by five goals in Russia and 1-2 at Highbury. Wolves fell 0-2 behind to Honved but came back after a Cullis half-time blast to win 3-2. Cullis apparently told his players to place even greater emphasis on their direct, long-ball game. He said to hit the long passes even longer, so that the wingers could get behind the Honved defence.

Chairman Joe Mears (left) presents Ted Drake with his championship medal (May 1955)

French club Lens welcome the new English champions. This programme has become a valuable collector's item

Moscow Dynamo players take the field at Chelsea bearing bouquets (November 1945).
(Below) Nearly 100,000 packed Stamford Bridge for the occasion

A baffled Moscow Dynamo skipper is shown the significance of tossing a coin
before kick-off. That is not the way the Soviets do things

Goalscorer supreme, Chelsea boss Ted Drake in his playing days

Bill Robertson, watched by Stan Wicks, clutches the ball during
a Sheffield Wednesday attack at Hillsborough (November 1954)

Les Stubbs (centre) is foiled by Sheffield Wednesday goalkeeper
Brian Ryalls in the same match, which ended 1-1

The bustle and excitement of another home match at Stamford Bridge

Teenage right-winger Peter Brabrook was called into the first team during Chelsea's championship run in

Ron Tindall

Centre-forward Ron Tindall signed
for Chelsea in April 1953 and scored
on his debut in November 1955

A scale model of Stamford Bridge as it was in the 1950s was displayed
in the stadium half a century later

Defender Ron Greenwood, who lost his
place in the Chelsea team and departed
during the championship season

Veteran John Harris was a hard man on
the field but a gentleman off it. He
played centre-half, then full-back

Little winger Frank Blunstone, possibly Ted Drake's shrewdest signing

Pre-War Stamford Bridge was a vast bowl, largely open to the elements

Roy Bentley (left), in World Cup action for England against Chile in Brazil in 1950.
England won 2-0 but four days later would be humiliated by the United States

CHELSEA

Colours—Shirts: Royal Blue (White Collars). Knickers: White. Stockings: Black, Blue and White Tops.

1. (Goal)
Robertson

2. (Right-back)   3. (Left-back)
Harris   **Willemse**

4. (Right-half)   5. (Centre-half)   6. (Left-half)
Armstrong   **Greenwood**   **Saunders**

7. (Outside-right)   8. (Inside-right)   9. (Centre-forward)   10. (Inside-left)   11. (Outside-left)
Parsons   **McNichol**   **Bentley**   **Stubbs**   **Blunstone**
(Captain)

Referee:
Mr. A. BOND
(London)

Linesmen:
Mr. C. B. BROOME (London)
[Red Flag]

Mr. W. E. DELLOW (Croydon)
[Yellow Flag]

Toth   **Szolnok**   **Palotas**   **Hidegkuti**   **Sandor**
                                             (Captain)
11. (Outside-left)   10. (Inside-left)   9. (Centre-forward)   8. (Inside-right)   7. (Outside-right)

Zakarias   **Kovacs (I.)**
6. (Left-half)   5. (Right-half)

Lantos   **Borzsey**   **Kovacs (J.)**
4. (Left-back)   3. (Centre-half)   2. (Right-back)

Olah
1. (Goal)

RED BANNER (HUNGARY)

Colours—Shirts: Blue. Knickers: White.

Because of similarity of colours, Red Banner have elected to play in all White.

Red Banner Reserves—FECSKE (Goal), KARASZ and MOLNAR (Forwards)

INJURIES: The goalkeeper may be changed at any time during the match, and substitutes will be allowed for any other players up to the 44th minute.

The line-up for the two teams when the Hungarian tourists played in December 1954

Nov. 1954: BENTLEY HAT-TRICKS WALES

Billy Wright introduces our captain to H.R.H. the Duke of Gloucester at the pre-match presentation.

Wales led 1-0 at half-time, then Bentley headed an equaliser (above) from Stanley Matthews' centre

*Roy outjumped King to head England's second goal, and this was the winner after Wales had equalised.
Bentley accomplished this treble in less than 15 minutes.*

Recalled by England, Bentley responds with a match-winning hat-trick against Wales

Stamford Bridge in the 1950s, complete with greyhound track and rickety North Stand

Soccer Star magazine could not resist this one last Chelsea joke after the title win (May 1955)

Roy Bentley leads the team out, followed by Frank Blunstone and Chick Thomson

Ken Armstrong earned one England cap   Chelsea, then struggling, won this game 4-1

Roy Bentley cracks home an early goal in the 3-1 win over Newcastle (September 1954)

Les Stubbs (centre) sees an effort sail over the bar at Hillsborough (November 1954)

Tottenham's Alf Ramsey concedes an early corner-kick under pressure from Roy Bentley. Chelsea won 2-1 (November 1954)

Chelsea inside-forward Len Goulden became manager at Watford

A rare goal by Ken Armstrong (right) against Aston Villa (November 1956)

Tony Nicholas (No 10) goes close at Villa Park (November 1956)

John McNichol is about to give Blackpool goalkeeper George Farm
a buffeting in a 0-0 draw at Stamford Bridge (March 1955)

Stan Willemse (No 3) clears off the line during Chelsea's 2-1 win
at Sheffield United (September 1954)

Popular winger Eric
Parsons was nicknamed
'the Rabbit'

Frank Blunstone was signed from Crewe   Peter Sillett's clearances inspired cartoons

" That's about the highest I've ever seen."

Les Stubbs heads the winning goal at Sheffield United (September 1954)

Bobby Smith (left) goes close with a glancing header at Newcastle (September 1954)

The Portsmouth Mail's cartoonist tells the story of Chelsea's visit (April 1955)

Chelsea fan Alan Scoltock unveils one of his 50-year-old souvenirs

Chelsea skipper and leading scorer Roy Bentley

Roy Bentley gets stuck in at Hillsborough in a 1-1 draw (November 1954)

Roy Bentley, out of picture, scores at Newcastle (September 1954)

CHELSEA 1954/55
Back Row; J.Oxberry (Trn), S.Willemse, K.Armstrong, P.Sillett, S.Wicks, C.Thomson, D.Saunders, J.Harris.
Front row: E.Parsons, J.McNichol, R.Bentley, T.Drake (Mgr), S.O'Connell, F.Blunstone.
Insets: W.Robertson, L.Stubbs.

Wolves goalkeeper Bert Williams somehow keeps out this Chelsea effort in a top-of-the-table clash (April 1955)

Eric Parsons (centre) puts Walsall under pressure in an FA Cup-tie
which Chelsea won 2-0 (January 1955)

Stan Wicks

Centre-half Stan Wicks
signed from Reading and
had to wait for his chance

Reliable wing-half Derek Saunders
was one of Chelsea's unsung heroes

Derek Saunders

John McNichol scores at Newcastle and collides with the cameraman (September 1954)

The Chelsea squad prepare for their end-of-season trip to the USA (May 1954)

Roy Bentley is on his way to a hat-trick in this thrilling 4-3 win over Newcastle
at Stamford Bridge (February 1955)

Chick Thomson makes a brave save in the 0-0 draw at home to Blackpool (March 1955)

Eric Parsons

Winger Eric Parsons proved to be a revelation after Ted Drake's arrival at Stamford Bridge

'From the bottom of our hearts, we say thank you.'
Roy Bentley addresses the fans (April 1955)

JUBILANT CROWDS THE CHAMPS

Cardiff Dash Last Hope Of Pompey

THE last lingering suspense is over. Chelsea are there ! For the first time in their 50 years' history they are League champions and at Stamford Bridge yesterday jubilant scenes greeted their triumph as wildly excited thousands surged in front of the stands calling for Manager Ted Drake and the men who had won the title.

Having seen their team gain a 3—0 victory over Sheffield Wednesday, the crowd had waited tensely for the one thing that could clinch Chelsea as title-holders . . the result of Portsmouth's match at Cardiff. Through it came.

Portsmouth had only drawn. Up went a mighty roar. Chelsea had done it.

"This is the happiest moment of my life," said broadly-smiling Ted Drake, who must surely have recalled his words to the directors when he was appointed manager at Stamford Bridge back in 1952. His comment then was : " Do not expect me to make Chelsea into a successful team for at least three years." Well, it's 1955 now, and Chelsea are the champs.

From the stands captain Roy Bentley spoke to the fans and told them: "I need not tell you how pleased we are, but we are pleased for you, too, because you have been behind us in other years."

Then soon, with cheers still ringing in their ears, the players returned to the dressing rooms, where they found a celebration case of champagne awaiting them.

Throughout the match the crowd had been kept informed of the progress of the game at Cardiff, and Portsmouth's Peter Harris must have caused many a Chelsea heart to miss a beat by scoring in the first three minutes. But, in the second half Cardiff's Roley Williams made himself a Stamford Bridge hero by scoring the equaliser. This killed Portsmouth's last possible hope of equalling Chelsea's points total.

To add to the drama at Stamford Bridge, McIntosh, the Sheffield Wednesday goalkeeper, was carried off on a stretcher after 55 minutes. He twisted ligaments in his back when falling awkwardly and was off for the rest of the game. Chelsea were leading 1—0 at the time and two more goals followed, including one from a Sillett penalty.

Now what about the other end of the First Division table? Well, Leicester beat Spurs in their relegation battle, which means that in six matches this month Tottenham have collected only one point. Still, Leicester will be lucky to escape the drop.

For the shock result of the day, over to Manchester City. The Cup-finalists, at one time a prospect for the Cup-League double, were beaten 6—1 on their own ground by Blackpool !

It was City's heaviest defeat of the season—and five of the Blackpool goals came in the second half. Perry hit a hat-trick, Mortensen netted twice, and, of course, Stanley Matthews was there providing openings.

Manchester's other team, United, scored a success by being the first side to win at Highbury since Nov. 13.

Those six clubs in the Second Division promotion shake-up did little to sort themselves out. It's still anybody's race. But Leeds now emerge as leaders through their 2—0 win over Blackburn, whose hopes now must be slim indeed. They drop to sixth in the table. Brook was the man who did the trick with four goals.

Birmingham lost ground, too, for at this vital time they could do no better than draw with Notts County at St. Andrews. It was only a goal in the dying minutes from Brown that saved Birmingham.

Ipswich still have slight hopes of escaping relegation, for while Plymouth were going down at Rotherham the East Anglian side took a point against Swansea. Luck was on the side of Ipswich for Swansea were handicapped by injuries.

Slight disappointment for Bristol City was that before a 27,000 crowd they failed to finish their home programme with a victory. But this was nothing compared to the triumph after the game when the City received their shield as champions of the Southern Section.

Leyton Orient, the side that once looked like finishing at the top of the Southern Section were in the day's second biggest shock match. Aldershot hit five against them, on the Orient's ground, too ! This makes five defeats in the last six games for Orient.

Barnsley, Accrington and York, top two of the Northern Section, all won, and if things keep going like this it will be Barnsley in the Second Division next season.

The News of the World reports an unlikely championship victory (April 1955)

This curious picture card has no name on the front or on the back.
Chelsea's No 4 was Ken Armstrong

'This is the happiest day of my life.' Ted Drake addresses the fans (April 1955)

Roy Bentley

Roy Bentley was one of the original roving centre-forwards. In addition to his 12 full England caps, he also represented Great Britain v Europe in 1955

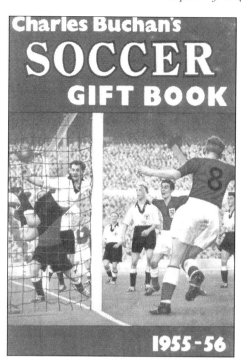

This popular annual featured Roy Bentley scoring at Wembley on its front cover

Roy Bentley takes a stroll down Memory Lane (May 2004)

The Times had predicted beforehand that if Wolves' long-ball style succeeded against Honved then it would surely catch on through the rest of British football. The purists weren't quite so convinced. Wolves relied on physical endeavour, fitness, a willingness to pass the ball long, high, and first time, and not dwell on it. It wasn't particularly easy on the eye, but it was usually effective. Cullis had no time for intricate, short-passing football. He was a disciple of speed, strength and directness. A disciplinarian very much of the old school, he had been a formidable sergeant major in the Army Physical Training Corps and his high standards when taking over Wolves in 1947 laid the foundations for their dominance of the 1950s. He ensured his Wolves players were fitter than anyone else and drummed into them the need to move the ball quickly out of defence.

Second Division West Ham could not emulate Wolves' triumph over the Continentals when they took on star-studded Milan at Upton Park the following day. The hapless Hammers were hammered 0-6. If this week's contests were to be treated as a best-of-three between England and Europe, the score now stood at one apiece and Stamford Bridge on 15th December would be the decider.

Special rules were laid down by the FA for Chelsea's game with Red Banner. The clubs were told that the goalkeeper may be changed at any time during the match and substitutes would be allowed for outfield players up to the forty-fourth minute but not beyond. Among the VIP guests for the big game was His Excellency Jozsef Katona, Minister of the Hungarian People's Republic.

The clash revived memories of the visit of Moscow Dynamo nine years earlier. That game had ended 3-3 and it was a big day, for it saw Chelsea pioneer the concept of post-War matches against top Continental clubs. On that day, the huge crowd burst the barriers, some gaining entry illegally and the attendance was estimated at 100,000. This time round, the crowd was somewhat smaller (40,452), perhaps due to the live TV coverage, but still high for a game kicking-off in the middle of a midweek afternoon. The match would turn out to be the last of its kind to be televised live without FA permission. Brighton and Watford, who had FA Cup replays that day, protested to the FA that their attendances were bound to be affected, and indeed they were.

There was much pre-match discussion over what tactics Red Banner might employ. The sixteen-page match programme warned spectators that the visitors' centre-half would probably carry No 3 on his back ('that is the habit with some of the continental teams'). A big talking point was exactly where the centre-forward would play. Red Banner's celebrated international No 9, Nandor Hidegkuti, may adopt what might be called 'backward-forward' tactics, warned the editorial. He had scored three at Wembley against England but only one in Budapest, when he played deeper, behind his fellow attackers. The article highlighted the fact that Roy Bentley was one of the first British No 9s to 'do the wandering act away from the middle of the field' in an effort to confuse his marker. Manchester City had latched on to this idea earlier in the season with the skilful Don Revie doing the same thing to great effect. The programme columnist also felt the need to warn spectators that Karoly Sandor liked to play with his shirt outside his shorts.

Several of the Hungary side who had defeated Scotland a week earlier were in the Red Banner line-up. Hungary had lost just once in fourteen games in the twelve months prior to this point, the solitary reverse being the shock defeat in the 1954 World Cup final to West Germany. The Chelsea programme quoted the national coach Gyula Mandi: 'My aim in training is to develop strength, suppleness and adroitness.' He told how his players practised the long and high jump, weight throwing, javelin, and steeple-chasing, plus swimming and other sports, and the leading clubs had physicians who helped get them into peak condition. Although Hungary's first football teachers were the English, they based their style on the Scots: 'The flat, combative Scottish game suited our people and our conditions much better,' said Sandor Barcs, President of the Hungarian FA. 'Our youngsters in those days did not learn on regulation pitches but on patches of waste ground with a rag ball or at best a tennis ball, sometimes 20-a-side. This meant the game was always rather "flat" and the players had to learn many tricks and devices.' Since those days the Hungarian system had been developed to reach a high standard. The proof lay in their appearance as well as their results – for they even looked more sophisticated than the Brits, playing in much shorter shorts and more modern-looking jerseys, for example.

Chelsea doubled normal admission prices for the occasion and the sense of anticipation was immense. However, the game itself turned into a huge disappointment after all the hype. There was little good football, and no sustained supremacy from the skilled Magyars, who seemed rattled by Chelsea's fierce tackling and muscular approach. The excitement of the Wolves v Honved encounter was not reproduced and the press widely condemned the two teams for excessive 'rough play and arguing with the referee.' *The Times* dismissed the match as a 'tasteless brew after the Molineux Champagne' and said the only sparks that flew came from hard Chelsea defensive tackling: 'This was no stroll in the sunshine for the Magyars and there were a few unseemly moments that needed a firmer control.' On a positive note, the Red Banner coach Gustav Sebes admitted to being impressed by wing-half Armstrong and was surprised he had not yet been capped.

The match had sprung to life on eighteen minutes when Hidegkuti headed past Robertson to round off a five-man move that had Chelsea chasing shadows. After this, Chelsea got stuck in and disrupted the Hungarians' smooth build-up. Five minutes before the interval, referee Mr A Bond – after checking with his linesman – decreed that Jozsef Kovacs had handled in a tussle with Blunstone and awarded a penalty. It was a borderline decision and enraged the visitors, who waved their arms in disgust and sent a torrent of dissent in Mr Bond's direction. It was several minutes before the gesticulating Hungarians could be persuaded to clear the area for the kick to be taken. Although unlikely to have sympathised with their sense of injustice, John Harris stroked a poor penalty well wide of the target. 'One's instincts said he had done so deliberately,' wrote the man from *The Times*. If so, times have changed, for deliberately missing seems unconscionable in front of a paying public.

A minute later, with the fans still perhaps debating whether or not the miss had been deliberate, Bentley headed a Parsons centre across goal to allow Stubbs to fire an equaliser. Chelsea tails were now up, and within another sixty seconds they went ahead. A Blunstone cross saw McNichol lash a shot goalwards, the ball rebounding for Bentley to flick calmly into the net.

Five minutes after half-time there was more penalty drama. Harris handled a dangerous Hidegkuti cross, but this time it was Mihaly Lantos who put his spot-kick wide. To astonishment all round, within a few minutes a third penalty was then missed. This time Borzsey pulled down the marauding Stan Willemse and Harris stepped up again, this time producing a firmer, more accurate kick, only to see it superbly saved by the diving figure of Karoly Olah, leaping to his left. It was the third penalty miss in eleven minutes of play, and for Chelsea their third successive failure from the spot.

Red Banner had lost their way since the first penalty incident and Chelsea looked 'dull and uninteresting' according to *The Times*, so it was a relief when a moment of inspiration arrived on the hour mark. The Hungarians created an equaliser to remember. At least ten passes were strung together in an elaborate move which ended with Hidegkuti gliding the ball through to Peter Palotas, who beat Robertson. One reporter said the move had been so long and intricate that it had seemed to start somewhere down the Fulham Road, wander off towards Walham Green, then finally end in the Chelsea net. The game ended 2-2, and despite the two fine Red Banner goals and all the penalty drama, was roundly criticised as a big disappointment by the next day's papers. Perhaps expectations had been a little too high at Stamford Bridge.

Traditionally, attendances are always down on the last Saturday before Christmas and a below-average 33,215 turned out for Chelsea's home game with struggling Leicester, even though Drake's men were by now on a run of seven unbeaten games, and back in the top four of the division. Parsons put them ahead against the Foxes, and the lead was extended by one of the strangest goals on record. Referee Arthur Ellis officially noted it as a 'joint own-goal'. As McNichol recalled years later: 'I hit the ball well, only for it to hit the underside of the bar and bounce on the goal-line. The two full-backs, [Jack] Froggatt and [Stan] Milburn, were so confused about what to do with the ball they both kicked it at exactly the same time and it went straight into the net – the only time I can remember an own goal being credited to two players. I was a bit disappointed they'd made contact really, as the ball was going to roll back into the net and be my goal, but it was real catalogue of errors and very funny to watch from a supporter's point of view.'

With Harris having missed three successive penalties, Bentley took responsibility when Chelsea got the chance to go 3-0 up – but to Stamford Bridge's collective horror he also failed, Leicester keeper John Anderson turning his effort around the post. Wasteful Chelsea had now missed four spot-kicks in succession. McNichol poached a third goal to give the scoreline a more realistic look, but Andy Graver sped past Ron Greenwood to bang home a late consolation for Leicester.

As usual, the players had no time sit to around unwrapping their presents, for their kick-off at Arsenal was scheduled for Christmas Day morning. The Gunners had several key men injured and gave a debut to young winger Danny Clapton, but it was former Chelsea hero Tommy Lawton who took centre-stage. Turning brilliantly, he cracked home a Wally Barnes pass for what proved the match-winner. It halted Chelsea's steady rise up the table but, undaunted, a massive crowd of 65,922 assembled at Stamford Bridge for the Boxing Day return and the gates were locked well before kick-off. In a tense and disjointed encounter, Derek Tapscott nicked an early goal against the run of play. Tom Whittaker's men battled bravely to resist Chelsea pressure, but conceded a second-half penalty. True to recent form, Bentley's effort was pushed over the bar by keeper Jack Kelsey. It was the team's fifth failure in a row, all coming in the past forty-four days. Then, just when it looked like Chelsea were doomed never to pierce the red and white barrier that confronted them, Roy Bentley headed down for O'Connell recalled for his first match since October – who cracked home a deserved equaliser.

This represented the club's final fixture of 1954, which had been a year of significant progress. Chelsea ended the calendar year fifth in the table, with several of their displays – notably that win at Wolves – proving they had what it took to beat the best. The squad looked as strong as any over recent years and was full of players who did their job effectively with a minimum of fuss and could consequently lay claim to the status of 'unsung hero'. Among this group were the likes of Les Stubbs, Ken Armstrong, and Derek Saunders.

Essex boy Stubbs, a hard-working inside-forward, had been signed from his home-town club, Southend United, two years earlier and was popular with fans for his all-action style. He tended to wave his arms like a windmill when turning and possessed a determined attitude and powerful shot. He provided beef in attack and was a useful foil for Bentley. It was usually Stubbs who made way when O'Connell was called up, but when he was the man in possession he invariably made a major contribution. Leaving school at fourteen, Stubbs had started work in a bicycle shop and it was Southend footballer Wilf Copping coming in to have his bike fixed which led to Stubbs making a career in football. Copping invited the youngster to Roots Hall for a trial. Stubbs' second stroke of luck was having his National Service duties postponed for six months because of an ankle injury. During that period his injury cleared up and he was offered a full-time contract by the seaside club. After the War he established himself as a prolific scorer at Roots Hall in Division Three (South) and after rumours about bigger clubs taking an interest, Chelsea took the plunge and paid £10,000 for his services in November 1952.

Another unsung hero who enjoyed a productive first half to 1954-55 was Armstrong, the only Chelsea man to be singled out for praise by the coach of the touring Red Banner side. Many felt this dependable half-back was by now ready for the senior England side, but to date he had earned just a handful of 'B' caps. Born in Bradford, he was a straight-talking, no-nonsense lad who was first spotted playing in a Sunday school team. His transfer from minor club Bradford Rovers to Chelsea cost one hundred guineas after a fellow soldier recommended him to then Chelsea manager Billy Birrell in 1945. Armstrong signed professional forms after being demobbed a year or so later, and went on to confirm that he was one of the greatest bargains ever picked up by the club. For a while he played in attack, but once Bentley arrived and settled in, Armstrong dropped back to his best position as right-half. He was a model of consistency and became a fixture in the side. He had sound positional sense and his tackling was firm and well-timed. He was the type of unfussy lynchpin that every side needed in the middle of the park.

Chapter 6

MOUNTING A SERIOUS CHALLENGE

(January-February 1955)

Chelsea's fierce tackling and physical commitment may have ruffled feathers among the visiting Hungarians in December, but the fall-out from that afternoon's events was nothing compared to the fuss created on New Year's Day 1955.

Ted Drake was unperturbed by the fact that his men were earning a tag for hard and uncompromising play on the field. And when they travelled north for the 1st January fixture with Bolton Wanderers – euphemistically regarded as an inhospitable place – he drummed into them the importance of not being intimidated by Bolton's reputation. To coin an old football cliché, he wanted his team to get their retaliation in first. This sort of talk was music to the ears of Chelsea hard-cases like Stan Willemse, John Harris and Derek Saunders. They loved nothing better than a good scrap.

Bolton, however, went into the contest plagued by injury worries. Key men were unavailable and they had to pitch rugged defender Malcolm Barrass into the forward line as an emergency measure in the hope that he might be able to unsettle the Chelsea defence and end Wanderers' run of four successive defeats. It was a desperate move and never likely to succeed, as things went from bad to worse for Bill Ridding's makeshift side. Roy Bentley admitted later that he had had a number of 'run-ins' down the years with Barrass: 'This time he didn't get near me all match after I told him before kick-off that I had his card marked. We ran Bolton ragged.'

Seamus O'Connell headed Chelsea in front after just four minutes and the home side never posed a serious threat from that moment onwards. Two goals by Bentley, plus success at last from the penalty spot – via full-back Peter Sillett – saw Chelsea cruise into a big lead as Bolton's misery deepened. Drake's men showed no mercy to their injury-hit opponents and had the partisan home crowd baying angrily at their robust tactics. The *Bolton Evening News* noted the next day that although there were free-kicks galore as Chelsea barged and elbowed into a 4-0 lead, the referee managed to miss many glaring offences. Reporter Haydn Berry considered that 'Far too much playing of the man went on and [Harold]

Hassall's injury further deepened the gloom that has descended on Burnden Park. He dribbled into a party of three Chelsea men, survived one foul and was met by Willemse as he tried to turn. Manager Ridding told me the knee-cap was torn out of position, a really bad injury. Hassall went straight to a nursing home and is probably out for the season ... Willemse came in for a certain amount of barracking from a crowd that frequently thought referee Parkhurst was too lenient. Play went on in an unpleasant atmosphere.'

The injury suffered by the five-times capped England international Hassall was indeed serious. There was extensive ligament damage and his knee-cap was badly dislocated. He needed immediate and lengthy surgery and would ultimately never play again. It was an unfortunate way for a skilful twenty-five-year-old's career to end. As they watched their popular inside-forward depart in agony on a stretcher, the home crowd turned viciously on Willemse, whose challenge had caused the injury. He was loudly jeered for the rest of the game and the hostile atmosphere intensified even further.

Hassall 'knew it was a bad one' straight away and had gestured frantically for those who rushed to his aid not to touch him. When trainer Bert Sproston arrived on the scene the player simply told him to get him on a stretcher and away to hospital as quickly as possible. Sproston was horrified by the sight of the damaged knee and later publicly congratulated the player for his cool-headedness. Hassall was also praised for sportingly not attributing blame to Willemse for his predicament. Hassall later related his version of events to the *Bolton Evening News*: 'I avoided one tackle, by Wicks I think, found the ball running a bit fast for me, with Willemse coming across to meet me. The ball still ran freely and I thought I might get through but Willemse ran with me for a yard or two and as I put my leg forward to reach the ball he tried to backheel it. My leg went between his and the next thing I was down, my knee hitting the ground a real wallop. It was not one of those deliberate breakfalls [sic] a player does to avoid injury; it was a real crash and I could see at once my kneecap was dislocated.'

Manager Ridding said: 'It must have been a fierce tear when that knee went and I have to hand it to Harold for the way he took it. That lad really is tough.' Asked if Chelsea had made enquiries about the player's condition since, Ridding said he had heard absolutely nothing from London, apart from a message from a girl supporter who thanked him for showing her party of supporters around the ground. After surgery to put his knee back together again, Hassall found himself on the same hospital ward as Bolton and England teammate Nat Lofthouse, who had also been under the surgeon's knife. Hassall was reportedly under the weather following his operation, but agreed to see reporter Berry, telling him he harboured no bad feelings towards Willemse: 'It was an accident and all over in a split second,' he said. Bolton fans were not so generous and Willemse received what the press described as 'not very complimentary' mail from Lancashire in the days after the game.

The local paper's tales of poor Hassall lying miserably in his hospital bed, listening to cricket commentary from Australia for hours on end, increased the anger felt by Bolton supporters who had been there to witness Chelsea's blood and guts display. Their anger was fuelled by comments from Ted Drake after the game, when, ludicrously, he claimed that Willemse was at least thirty yards from the incident that caused Hassall's misfortune. The crowd had been consoled a little near the end of the match when Barrass grabbed two consolation goals, but the game ended 5-2 to Chelsea and the beaten side now reported an injury list numbering seventeen men in all. What they did not yet know, of course, was that even worse news was to follow – Hassall would never play again.

Chelsea and Bolton had certainly conjured up some fierce battles over the years, but nothing quite compares with this one. Normally, Wanderers were the team dishing out the stick, but on this occasion Chelsea had met fire with fire. Years later, Jimmy Greaves would reflect on these contests: 'I used to hate going to Bolton [with Chelsea] – they were the hardest group of men you have ever come across in your life. Their ground at Burnden Park was a real scrapheap – if the crowd was getting at you, you used to hoof the ball onto the top of the stands and watch the rust fall on top of them. It was always 15 degrees below freezing and the pitch as hard as rock – and there would be little Drake's Ducklings. The Bolton lads would wait for us out on the pitch, wearing short sleeves, and say "Hey up, the pansies are up from London." They were frightening times, you couldn't wait to get into the cold shower and get home.'

Journalist and broadcaster Michael Parkinson was another famous name who reflected on the experiences of visiting players at Burnden Park in the 1950s. One day Bolton centre-forward Lofthouse took 'Parky' around the ground and showed him the track next to the pitch where full-back Tommy Banks liked to dump his victims, giving them 'a nice dose of gravel rash' into the bargain. According to Lofthouse, Banks' defensive partner Roy Hartle would call out: 'When tha's finished kicking thy man, Tommy, chip him over here so I can have a go at him.' Lofthouse added: 'I used to wear my shin-pads on the back of my calves with Tommy and Roy behind me. I would have hated playing against Banks and Hartle. I tell people that if Roy Hartle's mother had pulled on a No

11 shirt and run out at Burnden Park with the opposition, he would even have kicked her to death.'

Lifelong Bolton fan Les Dennis was tracked down to his home in Ireland and recalled the famous Battle of Burnden on New Year's Day 1955. 'I left Bolton to join the Royal Navy in 1946 and was only a very infrequent visitor to Burnden Park after I returned in late 1954. Consequently I saw Harold Hassall play just the once – in what, as I've always believed, was his very last game. [Willemse's tackle] happened near the touchline just in front of the Main Stand and my memory insists that I heard the crack of it from the railway terrace where I was standing, but that could be subconscious embroidery on my part! Hassall was said to be a clean-living lad who taught Sunday School at Walkden Congregational Church.'

Chelsea's warrior-like attitude of recent times came under the national microscope after this match, and few writers felt moved to defend them. One scribe, however, who did give them benefit of the doubt, was Michael Harvey of *Soccer Star* magazine. He said that Chelsea's growing reputation of being 'too vigorous' and prepared to 'win at all costs' was unjustified. They do play fighting football and defend forcefully, he wrote, but every tackle was a clean-spirited one. 'Willemse gets a lot of stick, but he's one of the best left-backs in England,' he added.

So what of Willemse? Was he really the ogre that he'd been painted? Like many so-called hard-men of football, he was said to be a charming fellow off the field. One writer even suggested that Willemse used to like sharing a bath with referees afterwards, chatting happily with them about the game just passed. Reminiscing about the 1954-55 season in later days, Willemse himself admitted he was never a classy player, but one who stuck to his task well and 'had a presence' on the pitch that meant his opponents worried about him and never took liberties. Referees took a far more lenient view of tackles from behind and shoulder-charging in those days, and as a result even bruisers like Stan rarely got booked. The player admitted that in the modern game he wouldn't last five minutes and would disappear under a flurry of yellow and red cards.

Willemse, born in Brighton, won county and international honours as a schoolboy footballer, but thoughts of a career in the game had to be put on hold while he served as a Royal Marine commando during the War. After being demobbed in 1946 he joined his home-town club as a £5-a-week professional . His career was again interrupted, this time by a mastoid operation which specialists feared might put a stop to his football for good, but typically he ignored their gloomy prognosis. He was transferred to Stamford Bridge in 1949 for a fee of around £6,000, the

Seagulls gratefully accepting funds they badly needed to finance the re-building work at the Goldstone Ground. In honour of this 'contribution' to the rebuilding, Willemse carved his initials into the wet concrete before disappearing to London. Commuting from the south coast, Willemse soon became an established member of the Chelsea side and even won international honours at England 'B' level.

After 1955 was ushered in with the controversial defeat of Bolton, Chelsea faced FA Cup action at Stamford Bridge on 8th January. Their third round opponents were little Walsall, languishing at the bottom of Division Three (South), but who were bound to raise their game for this crack at one of the big guns. Managed by Major Frank Buckley, the Saddlers duly put up a defiant display, but had no answer to the maraud-ing Bentley, who set up set up goals in each half for Seamus O'Connell and Les Stubbs. A 2-0 defeat was poor reward for some heroic individual Walsall displays, notably by veteran keeper Harry Baldwin, spirited little winger George Meek, and reserve defender Albert McPherson.

Meanwhile, Stamford Bridge was preparing to stage, on 19th January, the first Under-23 international to be played in this country, with England due to take on Italy. As became the fashion, the selectors made sure a 'home' player or two was in the line-up, to help swell the attendance, and Chelsea full-back Sillett was given the job of captaining England. The FA summoned the fourteen-man squad together at Highbury, but a burst of wintry weather meant this event was something of a wasted exercise. One paper jeered at the farcical nature of the whole thing, describing how some players had travelled long distances for the gathering, only to find an icy Arsenal pitch awaiting them, which meant all they did was have a meaningless twenty-minute kickabout in long trousers.

Adding to the farce, Chelsea's Frank Blunstone failed to arrive alto-gether and someone else pointed out that Doncaster's Ken Hardwick shouldn't be involved as he was well over twenty-three. The error was later corrected and Hardwick asked to step aside. The Chelsea grounds-man worked hard to get Stamford Bridge playable for the game and on a chilly night England triumphed 5-1. *The Times* praised Sillett for his cool distribution, although he was blamed for the solitary Italy goal. The bronzed young Italians strutted like ballet-dancers in lightweight footwear on the icy pitch, but it was the posturing of peacocks and they faded as the match went on, added *The Times*. When Chelsea's Blunstone swept home England's third goal, the contest was effectively over.

The middle Saturday of January was effectively wiped out by the bad weather, with forty-one senior games postponed in England and Scotland, including Chelsea's trip to Cardiff. The Football Pools cancelled their coupons for the week. Seven days later a dramatic thaw set in, which meant that many snow-covered pitches became waterlogged. There was also plenty of fog around and many more games were called off on 22nd January. Not all sport was disrupted by the weather though, and in the cosy surroundings of the Leicester Square Snooker Hall in Central London, 53-year-old Joe Davis put together the first-ever 147 break under match conditions on a standard table.

Chelsea's contest at home to Manchester City received a late go-ahead, but only after a pitch inspection. Chick Thomson was keeping goal for the first time this season in place of Bill Robertson, who had been injured in training. In quality, there was not much to choose between the two Chelsea keepers and Drake had few worries about throwing Thomson into the fray for his first taste of senior action in almost twelve months. Chelsea looked a little sluggish in the mud and had no answer to the prompting of Manchester City's deep-lying centre-forward Don Revie. Second-half goals by Joe Hayes and Roy Clarke gave City the points on a highly disappointing afternoon for Chelsea. Drake's men were not the first to be baffled that season by the so-called 'Revie Plan', and wing-half Derek Saunders recalled later that it was a strategy that generally baffled Drake. Most of the time Drake was a good tactician, said Saunders, but this was one of the few occasions he appeared completely outfoxed. Revie controlled the game from his deep position, and even though Chelsea knew exactly what was happening, it seemed there was nothing they could do about it.

Reward for Chelsea's Cup win over Walsall was a tough-looking tie at Second Division Bristol Rovers. Roy Bentley was delighted to be returning to the home of his first club, but was frustrated to succumb to a bout of tonsilitis just days before the game. The skipper was desperate to play in his home city and took to his bed in a bid to shake off the symptoms. Chelsea kept quiet about the situation and by the end of the week Bentley felt sufficiently recovered to assure Drake that he could play. The manager was delighted not to be losing his star player and publicly praised Bentley for his determination and dedication to the cause.

A record crowd of 36,000 squeezed into Eastville and Chelsea knew they would have their work cut out in such an atmosphere. However, the Pirates' giant-killing ambitions suffered a blow after just four minutes when a Blunstone cross was parried by keeper Howard Radford. The ball fell kindly for Parsons to score. That goal settled any Chelsea nerves and by half-time they were three up. In-form Blunstone set up McNichol for the second, and then drove home a fierce shot himself. Chelsea were in full command and Jack Pitt's penalty on the hour mark was academic.

Chelsea looked strong in central defence these days, with Stan Wicks settling down after his introduction in November. He was now Drake's first choice, ahead of the experienced Ron Greenwood, who had reached thirty-three and was seven years Wicks' senior. Greenwood was said to be aggrieved about being axed, but Drake stuck to his guns, feeling Wicks' extra fitness and sharpness fitted Chelsea's defensive requirements better than Greenwood's more thoughtful and measured approach.

Greenwood was not content to be out in the cold, believing he still had plenty to offer as a player, not to mention his coaching ambitions. He sought alternative pastures and by February 1955 neighbours Fulham had swooped for his signature. Greenwood had attended FA coaching sessions, alongside the likes of Bobby Robson and Jimmy Hill, and felt Fulham might be able to provide him a platform in this direction, in addition to giving him regular first-team football.

Bentley later recalled that Greenwood was a talented player, and if he had had the 'bite' of a Willemse, for example, would have made the perfect defender. Goalkeeper Thomson remembered Greenwood as a 'thinking man's footballer' who left the club under something of a cloud: 'When it was time for you to go, it was time for you to go,' reflected Thomson. Born in Burnley, Greenwood's family moved down to London when he was still a schoolboy. He played for local club Alperton against a Chelsea youth team and was one of a number from that team to be invited for trials at Stamford Bridge. These trials led to terms being offered to Greenwood, but the War and National Service intervened. After being demobbed, Greenwood found John Harris firmly established as Chelsea's centre-half and he was allowed to move to Bradford Park Avenue. Two seasons in Yorkshire were followed by four at Brentford and then, after turning down an offer from Plymouth, he rejoined Chelsea in October 1952. Shortly after his arrival, Jack Saunders was injured, allowing Greenwood to make his debut in the top division just a week or two short of his thirty-first birthday. His bow came in front of a 60,000 crowd at home to Tottenham.

A year or so into his second spell at Chelsea, Greenwood experienced an event that made him 'see the light' and which changed his life. On 25th November 1953, he took his seat at Wembley Stadium, close to the Royal box, and watched in astonishment as an England side – with just one defeat in its previous twenty-one games – were taught a football lesson by Ferenc Puskas and his Hungarian teammates. Greenwood told the *Daily Mail* later:

'[Hungary's display] was an exercise in wit. Perhaps without realising it, I had been waiting for someone to show me the way. When the proof came that afternoon, it was as if someone had removed the scales from my eyes. All my basic ideas on the game suddenly came together. Though the result [Hungary won 6-3] was written up like a national disaster, for me it was a new start. The Hungarians played a system we had not seen before – 4-2-4. Their centre-forward played in a deep position thirty yards away from England's centre half. But the most impressive feature was their teamwork. Watching them rip England apart had a profound effect on me. The Hungarians simply played football differently. They used another language. Their game was based on the short pass, although they were always ready with a long one when the moment was right. They kept the ball on the ground and fizzed it about. Their pace was tremendous and they moved with cunning and intelligence.'

A few months after this Wembley eye-opener, Greenwood began developing his interest in tactics and coaching by accepting the chance to coach US airmen based at Woodbridge in Suffolk, working alongside Cambridge City coach Roddy Munroe. This interest in the technical side of the game would blossom in a big way – more of which later.

In early February 1955 Chelsea headed north to face Everton, just one place behind them at seventh in the League table. Goalkeeper Thomson was pleased to find that his first away game in almost a year would be in front of the Goodison fans, because he always enjoyed trips there. Every visit would see him receive a bag of Everton toffees from an old woman who always stood behind the goal. Thomson recalled: 'She was a dear old soul who always stood just behind my left post, but it seemed as if everyone else behind that goal enjoyed giving the opponents' goalie a tough time.'

Thomson relished his toffees after Roy Bentley's header helped Chelsea to a 1-1 draw and kept them in sixth spot. The supply of sweets was nearly curtailed on a subsequent visit to Goodison. Thomson recalled how a Johnny McNichol shot flew behind the Everton goal and smashed a flask of tea belonging to an Everton supporter. When the teams swapped ends, Thomson arrived between the posts to overhear the irate flask-owner ordering the woman not to hand over any toffees to any Chelsea players!

By mid-February, Wolves remained most pundits' favourites to retain the League title, but Stan Cullis's all-star side had not opened up a big lead and the race was still wide open. All the clubs in the top ten were in with a shout, and this certainly included Chelsea, who were sixth with two-thirds of the season gone.

Few newspaper column inches in February were occupied by the title race, however, for the favourite topic was the way wing maestro Stan

Matthews was playing as well as ever, despite having passed his fortieth birthday. The Blackpool and England star was still entrancing fans up and down the country with his marvellous ball control, and the characteristic way with which he beat his full-back. Matthews' method involved almost ambling up to his opponent, touching the ball from one foot to the other, elbows hanging loose, and then zipping past in a flash, usually drawing in another opponent before crossing the ball straight to Stan Mortensen's head. Everyone knew the Matthews style and his tricks, but few could do much about them. He was regarded as the fastest man in the country over short distances and a full-back would know he was in trouble every time Stan's teammates managed to ping the ball straight to his feet, as opposed to merely knocking it down the flank. Chelsea, of course, had two fine wingers themselves, in Blunstone and Parsons, but Matthews at the time was still in class by himself.

Chelsea fans relished a goal feast on 12th February when attack-minded Newcastle United came to town. And they weren't the only ones. In forty-five League games that day, 178 goals were scored (an average of roughly four per game), with fifty-nine in the eleven First Division matches (average 5.36). By now, Blackburn had amassed ninety-seven goals in just thirty matches in the Second Division and their centre forward Tommy Briggs even managed seven in one game, against Bristol Rovers.

Bentley put Chelsea ahead against Newcastle, following a blunder by diminutive keeper Ronnie Simpson, whereupon the Geordies were hit by a three-goal-in-four-minutes blast in the second half. This purple patch saw Bentley complete his first hat-trick of the season and, perhaps understandably, after the fourth goal went in, Chelsea took their foot off the gas. The visitors took advantage and launched an almighty late fight-back, Vic Keeble bagging two goals and Jackie Milburn also netting to bring the score to 4-3. By the end, Chelsea were hanging on desperately in scenes reminiscent of the Manchester United game in October, only this time with the roles reversed.

Chelsea's outside hopes of capturing the League title were put on the back burner for a week when the side travelled to Notts County for a fifth round FA Cup-tie with the Second Division side. The treacherous, icy pitch was an ideal leveller and County approached their giant-killing task with relish. Ron Wylie skilfully set up Albert Broadbent for a 51st-minute goal which proved to be the winner. Chelsea's best chance of staying in the Cup fell to Parsons, but the speedy winger made a hash of an open goal, which meant Chelsea were out for another year. County's reward was a quarter-final tie at home to little York City of the Third Division

(North), but this golden opportunity to reach the semi-finals would be passed up. The defiant Minstermen would shock Meadow Lane by winning 1-0 with a goal from Arthur Bottom.

Chelsea reacted positively to the misery of their Cup defeat, bouncing back a week later to hammer Huddersfield Town 4-1 at Stamford Bridge, a result that saw them soar into third place in Division One, and raised, for the first time, serious hopes of a title challenge. The afternoon had started off badly, for Chelsea went in at half-time a goal down to Gerald Burrell's effort and not looking in great shape. The second period was a different story and Town's defence was breached four times – the best of the goals being an astonishing effort from Bentley, who returned a Jack Wheeler goal-kick first time from forty-five yards, the ball sailing into the net to make it 3-1. Wheeler was so stunned that seconds later he made a hash of things and Stubbs grabbed a fourth.

Chelsea's inconsistency was certainly still evident over the course of the season as a whole, but they had nevertheless got themselves into a challenging position and were one of several serious contenders in a congested top half of the table. After beating Huddersfield they were a mere three points behind leaders Wolves, both clubs having played thirty games. Sunderland were second, two points ahead of Chelsea. Wolves and Sunderland had yet to visit Stamford Bridge, which meant an intriguing run in.

Many supporters of the time were all too familiar with Chelsea's frustrating habit of promising much and delivering little, however, and refused to get carried away. Better to just enjoy things while they were going well, seemed to be the general attitude. Or, to coin a well-worn phrase, 'take each match as it comes.' It was only a game after all.

For the small boys of the 1950s, First Division football was not merely a game, it represented an exciting splash of colour to light up the gloom of a post-War winter. Richard Posner remembers his match-day experiences of the time:

'My father would drive from home and we would park in one of the streets near the Chelsea ground. There were no meters, no restrictions, but it was still difficult to find a space nearby and normally led to a 20-30 minute walk. As we locked the car, we would always be approached by a young lad: "Look after your car, sir?" My Dad always said yes, not out of fear of having it damaged by the lad, but simply out of generosity. I didn't have a wooden rattle, although many fans did, but I did wear a blue and white scarf which my mother knitted for me, plus a Chelsea rosette. Our season tickets were in the old East Stand, Block E, Row B – the best seats just to the right of the players' tunnel and adjacent to the Directors

Box. I'd buy a programme for 6d [that's six old pence] which I'd read from cover to cover while Dad went to the bar at the top of the stand – alcohol was served so kids weren't allowed. The Chelsea programme was without doubt the best in the country; it had no adverts and for 6d you got sixteen pages of news, facts and pictures.

'Often the programme would recount tales of outstanding goalscoring feats of youth or reserve team players. I remember either Barry Smart or Colin Shaw once scoring eight goals in one reserve game; I don't think Barry ever played for the first team, while Colin did, but never really made the grade. Once I'd read the programme, I'd place it carefully on my seat and sit on it for the duration, thereby ensuring that I could get it home crease-free and in perfect condition so that I could read it again and again.

'There was generally much less hostility at matches in those days. Bad language was never heard and there was no organised singing or chanting. The crowds were still very partisan of course, but there was little of the aggression that you get today. Having said that, I remember going to one of my first ever away games, a third round FA Cup match at Leyton Orient [January 1957]. When we had a corner, the ground erupted with whistles and boos, and I remember asking my father why they were doing that. I also remember an away game at West Ham when Phil Woosnam was carried off after a foul by one of our players; when he returned to the field the noise was unbelievable, and the aggression showed to one little boy with a Chelsea rosette was quite terrifying.

'After a game had finished my dad and I would trudge, disconsolately usually, back to the car where we were met by the car's minder. "Some kid jumped on the bonnet, sir, but I kicked him off." My dad would smile as he gave him his tip and I would be amazed at such feats of courage from one so young. Before we got home we'd buy the classified editions of the three, yes three, London evening papers, *Star*, *News* and *Standard*, to read the match reports, although we already knew the results from listening to Sports Report on the radio. How on earth were the papers printed and delivered in such a short space of time in the pre-computer days?'

Unlike Richard Posner, Alec McKay was one of the many thousands who did not have the advantage of a lift in a car to the ground, or access to the best seats. He remembers: 'I lived in Kilburn and either caught the 31 or 28 bus, depending on which one came first. I always had fish and chips before I left and never ate anything at the ground. The crowd was a little older than it seems in modern times, but that may be because I was so young then. Although they were noisy, there did not seem to be many hooligans around and I never saw any punch ups between supporters although there was some banter between the fans. I remember the toilet facilities were dire and at half time and full time I tried to avoid them if possible. I always bought a programme and always wore a rosette or Chelsea colours in some form. I also had a royal blue and white Chelsea scarf.'

Alan Scoltock was not content with just seeing his heroes on match-days, for he would visit the Stamford Bridge area to try and get a glimpse of the players in midweek, too. He recalled: 'I used to see the players when they came and went from the café on the corner of Billington Road nearby, over the bridge, where they would go and play snooker. They would train on the pitch at Stamford Bridge and would finish around mid-morning – about 11.30 – and we would be waiting outside. Attendances that season would fluctuate – for I seem to recall that many fans would pick and choose which games to go to. There was always attractive football from Chelsea but they were very inconsistent usually, and it was totally out of character to become a serious contender for the title by the time March came around.

'I remember them climbing the table after Christmas 1954 and they were not a bad side at that point. The biggest matches of all were always our London derbies involving Arsenal and Tottenham. We were always seen as a bit of a showbiz club, although the supporters were mostly ordinary working-class people. Quite a few fans were like me and would go to Chelsea one week and Fulham the next. I used to cycle to games and for sixpence you could put your bike in a reasonably safe back garden near the ground. It cost about 2s 6d to get into the game. We would congregate in Chelsea on the Saturday morning and then go down to the ground about 1.30 or 2pm, wearing our scarves and colours. We'd generally get in at about 2.15pm and it would all be very exciting, particularly that moment when you'd suddenly emerge to see the bright green grass on the other side of the dog track.'

Chapter 7

TO THE TOP OF THE PILE

(March 1955)

Following the handsome wins over Newcastle and Huddersfield, it took a soft goal by Northern Ireland international Peter McParland to knock Chelsea's title challenge off the rails again. That late goal capped a 2-3 defeat by mid-table Aston Villa on 5th March and was hard for Ted Drake to swallow, for it was down to a blunder by Chick Thomson. The goalkeeper had flapped at a cross and palmed the ball straight to the feet of twenty-year-old winger McParland, who made no mistake.

So, with ground to make up again, Chelsea faced another contest in the Midlands four days later. This re-arranged fixture at relegation-threatened West Bromwich Albion would have to be won to re-establish Chelsea among the title-challenging pack. Their chances suffered a blow when full-back Stan Willemse announced that he felt unwell and was diagnosed as having a nasty bout of flu. Drake sent him and his wife to a seaside hotel in Folkestone at the club's expense, in order to recuperate. For the West Brom fixture, veteran John Harris was recalled in Willemse's place, although with the region hit by snowfalls, the match itself looked in jeopardy.

Referee Webb inspected the Hawthorns turf on the Wednesday morning and declared the pitch playable, although there was plenty of snow and certain areas seemed dangerously slippery. Many home fans clearly felt the game had little chance of going ahead for fewer than 8,000 turned up, although, of course, low attendances were expected for all midweek afternoon kick-offs. FA Cup-holders Albion, belying their lowly League placing, started like a train in the tricky conditions and Chelsea were stunned midway through the first half by conceding two goals in a minute. Playing without his injured strike partner Johnny Nichols, the redoubtable Ronnie Allen pounced twice to leave Chelsea reeling.

Allen, who had scored twice to help West Brom defeat Preston North End in the 1954 FA Cup final, had partnered Chelsea's Roy Bentley in England's 3-1 victory over West Germany earlier in the season, and was still on top of his game. This ebullient son of the Potteries was well short of 6ft tall and weighed barely 11st. This meant he hardly fitted the pattern of the dreadnought centre-forward favoured for so long in the

English game. Allen relied less on physique than on skill, flair, speed of movement, and thought. He had also scored against Chelsea earlier in the campaign in the 3-3 draw at Stamford Bridge, at a time when West Brom were sitting proudly at the top of the table. Their subsequent collapse had been dramatic, but at the Hawthorns in March the icy pitch was proving to be a great leveller.

Two goals in arrears, the tide only began to turn for Chelsea in the last half-hour. Out of the blue, wing-half Derek Saunders strode forward and tried his luck from twenty yards, the ball sailing into the net past his near-namesake, Sanders, in the Albion goal. The nature of the game changed in that instant with Chelsea now glimpsing their chance to salvage something. With ten minutes remaining, full-back John Sillett marched up to take a free-kick just outside the Albion area. His fierce drive was deflected in by a defender to bring the scores level. Vic Buckingham's side were visibly crumbling and it was no surprise when Chelsea took the lead two minutes later. Keeper Sanders clashed with Les Stubbs and a penalty was awarded. Sillett fired it home with his usual composure and lack of fuss. To rub salt into Albion wounds, Bentley made it four near the final whistle. The scoreline represented a superb comeback, and Chelsea's four-goal burst in the final twenty-six minutes put their title challenge back on track. They were now third, three points behind Wolves.

Winger Frank Blunstone later pinpointed that afternoon in the West Midlands as the pivotal moment, when the team began to emerge as serious contenders. He said Stubbs had won the game for Chelsea that day, not through scoring or doing anything spectacular, but by his less obvious contribution of hard work and persistence. Blunstone recalled that Stubbs spent the ninety minutes 'niggling' at Albion keeper Jack Sanders and unsettled him to the extent where, at one point, he lost his temper, kicked the ball away, turned round and lashed out at Stubbs, thus conceding the crucial 82nd-minute penalty. Blunstone remembered that the game was played in dreadful conditions and would never have been allowed to start in modern times. Passing was a lottery in the thick snow and through balls would often stop dead and players would have to chase after their own passes to win the ball back all over again. He said the players started to get really excited about the run in to the end of the season after their West Brom victory, but recalled that manager Drake's attitude and demeanour remained the same despite the increase in pressure and expectation.

What Chelsea now needed, to underline their claim as serious challengers, was an emphatic home performance against another side battling relegation, Blackpool. A healthy 55,227 crowd packed into Stamford

Bridge expecting Chelsea to punish their attractive but struggling opponents. As has happened so many times before and since at the Bridge, expectation exceeded delivery. It was a dreadful game. Chelsea's shot-shy forwards looked anxious and the occasion was not even graced by anything spectacular from England winger Stan Matthews. The forty-year-old kept full-back Sillett on his toes, but was unable to carve out many chances. Afterwards Matthews was complimentary about Sillett's abilities, but this was scant consolation after the dropping of a precious point. Many of the crowd gave up the ghost long before the final whistle and made their way home, sensing this was not going to be Chelsea's day and that a goalless draw was inevitable.

The point gained from this disappointing afternoon was, however, enough to push Chelsea into second place behind Wolves – their highest placing of the season. Wolves had played fewer games, on account of the flurry of winter postponements, but still had to travel to Stamford Bridge, of course. The failure to score against Blackpool forced Drake to reassess his forward options for the next match – the short trip to Charlton Athletic – the outcome being that he brought back amateur Seamus O'Connell in place of Stubbs. O'Connell had been a shining star for Bishop Auckland but would be available to Chelsea if selected. Drake valued O'Connell's flair and incisive finishing ahead of the graft and commitment that Stubbs could offer. The switch paid off. O'Connell made one of his rare visits to London to earn 'man of the match' plaudits at The Valley. He linked up neatly with Blunstone to allow the winger to slot home the opening goal after just twelve minutes.

Later in the game, with Jimmy Seed's side pressing for an equaliser, their popular forty-one-year-old long-serving goalkeeper Sam Bartram went on one of his infamous 'walkabouts'. He was caught well out of his area by a McNichol effort, but centre-half Frank Ufton scrambled back to clear. It was a great opportunity spurned to put the game beyond Charlton's reach. Moments later, however, O'Connell chested down a Ken Armstrong pass and lashed the ball home to make sure of the two points. On the balance of play it had not been an emphatic victory, but Chelsea had taken their chances efficiently and defended solidly at the other end.

The battle at the top was now certainly hotting up. On 19th March, Wolves failed to force a win at home to Newcastle, and the day's results left Chelsea still in second place, one point behind, but having played a game more. One concern for Ted Drake at this time was the continuing absence of Willemse, who had still not recovered from his dose of flu. Willemse had been particularly sore at missing the Charlton game as he had enjoyed past meetings with the Addicks, particularly the confrontations with menacing thirty-year-old winger Gordon Hurst. Reminiscing about these battles, Willemse said he recalled 'taking Hurst out twice' in one game, which led to the Charlton fans getting on his back 'booing and calling me all the names under the sun'. According to Stan's story, the referee marched over, wagging his finger and pretending to give Willemse a stern ticking off, in order to appease the Charlton supporters. With Willemse joining in the fun and hanging his head like a chastened school-boy, the referee asked him if he was going to the races the following Monday? When Stan replied that he was, the ref allegedly replied: 'OK, well cut that out and I'll see you at the first race then.'

The antics during the Charlton match of home goalkeeper Sam Bartram – making heroic saves one minute and being stranded hopelessly out of position the next – surprised nobody. Here was one of the game's great characters, a hugely popular figure who loved to keep the fans entertained. And this was not the first occasion that he had livened up a Charlton-Chelsea game either. In his autobiography, *Sam Bartram by Himself* (1956), he wrote:

'Soon after the kick-off [fog] began to thicken rapidly at the far end, travelling past Vic Woodley in the Chelsea goal and rolling steadily towards me. The referee stopped the game, and then, as visibility became clearer, restarted it. We were on top at this time, and I saw fewer and fewer figures as we attacked steadily. I paced up and down my goal-line, happy in the knowledge that Chelsea were being pinned in their own half. The boys must be giving the Pensioners the hammer, I thought smugly, as I stamped my feet for warmth. Quite obviously however, we were not getting the ball into the net. For no players were coming back to line up, as they would have done following a goal. Time passed, and I made several advances towards the edge of the penalty area, peering through the murk which was getting thicker every minute. Still I could see nothing. The Chelsea defence was clearly being run off its feet. After a long time a figure loomed out of the curtain of fog in front of me. It was a policeman, and he gaped at me incredulously. "What on earth are you doing here?" he gasped. "The game was stopped a quarter of an hour ago. The field's completely empty." And when I groped my way to the dressing-room the rest of the Charlton team, already out of the bath, were convulsed with laughter.'

The two points gleaned from The Valley on 19th March had certainly returned the smiles to the faces of Blues supporters, and although the press generally concurred that Chelsea did not really have the look of true champions about them, they were certainly putting the heat on favourites Wolves, whose own recent form had been shaky. At this stage, a serious betting man would probably not have wagered against Wolves, but on paper Chelsea were certainly in with a great chance of upsetting the apple-cart. Both clubs faced a run-in involving several midweek afternoon games, the result of winter postponements. On 23rd March, Chelsea had to venture into South Wales to face Cardiff City, knowing that victory would put them top of the League for the first time since the War.

In front of a paltry crowd of under 17,000, Chelsea registered another Wednesday afternoon success, the only goal of a disjointed contest coming from that man O'Connell. He struck two minutes before the interval to register his seventh goal in seven Chelsea games as an amateur player. It took a dogged rearguard display after the break to keep the lead intact but Chelsea somehow survived and the group of players who made their way back to London on the train afterwards were in high spirits. Chelsea were top of the table, and although the realists among their fans thought it probably wouldn't last, it was still a moment to be celebrated. Some newspapers excitedly suggested this was the club's first ever taste of life at the summit, but they had in fact briefly been in pole position in 1922 and in 1937.

Exactly how close were Chelsea to their first championship in fifty years? Wolves were one point behind, but had two games in hand, meaning they remained favourites. But Stan Cullis's side had gone off the boil. Just now they seemed as inconsistent as Chelsea. Life was good for the long-suffering Stamford Bridge fans and they lapped up the press coverage of the strange state of affairs at the top of the League. Showbiz club Chelsea top of the pile – surely there's been some mistake? No, there it was in black and white on all the sports pages.

But then – two days after the Cardiff victory – those reassuring sports pages disappeared altogether! On 25th March, all British national newspapers were hit by strike action. The first editions were lost on the Friday morning and there would be no more papers at all for the next twenty-six days. No longer could Chelsea fans sit and gaze dreamily at the League table, with their boys proudly printed in the No 1 position. Some wags even suggested that Chelsea's success was the reason for the strike, as the union leader was an Arsenal fan who couldn't bear to read about it!

Probably the most exciting and important few weeks in the club's history were about to unfold and there would be no press coverage to keep the long-suffering fans abreast of developments. The strike involved maintenance electricians and engineers, locked in dispute with the Newspaper Proprietors' Association over a pay offer. The Amalgamated

Union of Engineering Workers and the Electrical Trades Union had rejected the pay offer, claiming they had fallen behind pre-War levels. These two rebel unions had countless members working in national paper offices and their action brought Fleet Street to its knees.

Meanwhile, a few miles to the west of troubled Fleet Street, Chelsea boss Ted Drake was mulling over his plans for the crucial visit of Sunderland to Stamford Bridge on the afternoon of Tuesday, 29th March. O'Connell had picked up an injury playing for Bishop Auckland and would not be available, and neither would winger Blunstone, who was away on England duty. Drake sprang a major surprise by calling up untried youngster Peter Brabrook to take O'Connell's place, and asking full-back Willemse to play in Blunstone's position. Willemse was still taking the Folkestone sea air in a bid to shake off his flu when he received Drake's phone call. The manager sought reassurances that he hadn't overdone the resting and lost his fitness completely, before inviting the surprised Stan to get across to SW6 and pull on the No 11 shirt – a position he had never played before.

So, with a raw seventeen-year-old at inside-left and a semi-fit full-back playing on the wing outside him, Chelsea prepared for one of the most important games in their history. Opponents Sunderland still harboured their own title hopes. They were two points behind and knew that defeat at Stamford Bridge would probably spell the end of their chances. For Chelsea it was a must-win situation, and they had the crowd on its feet in the early stages with some sustained attacking. Within fifteen minutes they had surged two goals ahead and the points looked secure. Brabrook looked far from overawed and it was his firm cross that was hooked into his own net by Joe MacDonald for an own-goal on eleven minutes. Three minutes later there was an almighty roar as the returning Willemse, enjoying his debut in attack, scored only his second goal for the club in what was his 150th League and Cup game. There was understandable glee from the man himself, and the celebrations lasted several minutes after he cracked the ball home when Sunderland keeper Bill Fraser failed to hang on to a corner-kick. Although Chelsea failed to find the net again, they looked the better side for much of the game, but had to suffer worrying moments after Charlie Fleming blasted home on fifty-three minutes to halve the deficit. The 2-1 win stretched Chelsea's lead at the top to three points, although all the challengers behind them had at least one game in hand.

It was a great day's work, but the press were not over-impressed. According to *The Times*: 'Chelsea as much resembled prospective champions as the Battersea Power Station looks like a painting by Cezanne.'

It had been a dream debut for Greenwich-born teenager Brabrook, who had come up through the club's junior ranks. He had started out as an outside-right with East Ham, Essex and London Schoolboys, and was spotted by West Ham. But the Hammers' manager, Ted Fenton, only offered Brabrook two nights training per week instead of the full-time groundstaff place the youngster coveted. West Ham's loss was Chelsea's gain, because Chelsea scout Jimmy Thompson also liked what he saw. Shortly afterwards Brabrook impressed again by lashing in two goals for London Boys against West Germany at Highbury. On returning home to Greenwich he found the persuasive Jimmy Thompson waiting for him. Brabrook signed on the dotted line and West Ham were soon ruing their reluctance to make him a better offer. Brabrook had barely progressed to the reserve side by the time Drake called on him for his March 1955 senior debut, but he repaid the manager's faith with a fine display, and even did enough to keep his place for the next two important games.

Centre-half Stan Wicks was another newcomer to the first team that season, of course, but the big defender was almost ten years older than Brabrook and had five years' experience with Third Division (South) Reading under his belt. As the season's run-in intensified, Wicks was another player who justified the faith shown in him by the manager. His displays were steady and reliable and he was a tower of strength in the air. He may have been a bit 'rough round the edges' compared to Ron Greenwood, the man he replaced, but Wicks did a sterling job in early 1955 against some star-studded forward lines. The five-figure fee paid to Reading looked decent value for a man who had already played for England 'B' [in a 1-7 defeat by France Espoirs in May 1952] while still on the Berkshire club's books.

As the title race gathered momentum in late March it was becoming clear that Drake's bargain buys from the lower divisions were repaying their transfer fees many times over. In addition to Wicks and Blunstone, another example of this was inside-right Johnny McNichol. Hailing from the Kilmarnock area, McNichol started his working life as a shop assistant and then an apprentice motor mechanic and only played local football. After his National Service ended, it was on the cards that McNichol would join Kilmarnock until an unexpected invitation from Newcastle intervened. He played in a public trial match before a big crowd and was offered a deal by the Magpies. They allowed him to play as an amateur while completing his apprenticeship: his duties involved guarding the Rolls-Royces at a local undertakers. In the summer of 1948 McNichol was considering an offer from Newcastle to turn professional when Brighton came along dangling the carrot of more money if he dropped two divisions. The £12-a-week pay-packet was too tempting and he headed south where four excellent seasons at the Goldstone followed. To this day, old-time Seagulls supporters reckon McNichol to have been Albion's best inside-forward since the War.

Against Newport County, McNichol equalled a club record by scoring four in a 9-1 win. It might have been six had his teammates been more generous and allowed him to take the two penalties awarded to Brighton. McNichol became Ted Drake's first signing as manager of Chelsea for £12,000 in an exchange deal that took Jimmy Leadbetter to Sussex. McNichol was an instant hit at Stamford Bridge and enjoyed commuting from his Brighton home up to London for training. Having registered for several FA coaching courses before his arrival, he was surprised at the poor basic standard of training at Chelsea. He often felt he could have organised better sessions himself, but recognised that Drake was more of an 'up-and-at-'em' character, rather than a well-organised strategist. He nevertheless had enormous respect for Drake and got on well with him from the start. He recalled that their only falling out would come later on, when McNichol opened a newsagent's shop in Brighton, which meant he had to do several hours work before his morning training session, a lifestyle that did not seem to improve his football.

Meanwhile, as April dawned with the team top of the League, this was a time of high excitement for Chelsea fans. Tony Banks remembers the long weeks without newspapers when supporters had to do without their 'fix' of football news: 'We had to get the news through the radio, for not that many people had TV in those days. I don't think my family had a set at that time. To get to the games in those days I would usually take the No 45 bus from Brixton where we lived to the north side of Battersea Bridge and then go through Lotts Road. Sometimes I would cycle. You would get to the ground and there'd be tea, Bovril and meat pies sometimes available outside, but I can't remember much being on sale inside. The toilet facilities were very primitive indeed, for the men it was just these open sheds. I'm not sure what there was for women, but some women did go to games, although not as many as today. It was very much a working class man's sport then and facilities in general were very basic. Match programmes were popular and I would get one at every game and slip it inside my jumper to prevent it getting creased. I went to every game and got the whole set in 1954-55 and still have them to this day.

'I had first started going in the period 1951-52, but 1954-55 was the first time I went to every game. I often went on my own although sometimes with my dad, or the odd mate. A youngster going off alone by bus or cycle would be very difficult these days but in those times parents were not worried and there seemed to be no problems. The souvenirs and favours around were scarves, rosettes, rattles and lapel badges, plus a bob-ble hat in winter. But these would not come from the type of Megastore the club has got now, in fact there was no shop at all, for you'd get things from blokes in the street or your mum would knit you a scarf. I remem-ber one vendor who would always be there and would sell old pro-grammes and photos of the players. Kids would literally be rolled over the heads of the adults to the front so they could see. At the games with huge crowds some people would climb up the scoreboard to get a better view and nobody would seem really worried about the dangers. Most people seemed to show good sense and they didn't have a problem accommodating huge attendances. They would use "crowd packers" for the big days, to supervise things and keep the aisles clear. It was very much a working class game in 1955 and it was like a social occasion going to football really. Although I often went alone you would go to your favourite spot and recognise all the folk around you, even though you may not know their names and you were among friends. People liked to stand on the same spot to see the games and you have to remember most of them had their football, but very little other entertainment. The local area, including Fulham, was very working class in those days, so the peo-ple who went to games reflected the local population.'

It is strange to think that Tony Banks, a future Government Minister, and John Major, a future Prime Minister, were both excited small boys in the crowd at Chelsea during this period. They shared a passion for the club that endures to this day, even though they would later be on oppos-ing sides of the political spectrum.

Hansard, which records debates in the House of Commons, contains material that paints a colourful impression of these two famous Chelsea fans' childhoods. In a session from January 1993, Banks is reported thus: 'What on earth does [PM John Major's] phrase [get back to basics] mean? If the Prime Minister has in mind a golden age it must mean Brixton and getting back to the basics of the 1950s. I can connect easily with that sort of image because I was also brought up in Brixton in the 1950s. We lived in a London county council home. The Majors, of course, lived in a pri-vately rented mansion flat, as I understand, and we always used to envy them greatly. They were well-known nobs in the area, Mr. Deputy Speaker, I can tell you. It was, however, a time of great security, I am sure, for both of us although, mercifully, we were blissfully unaware of each other's existence.

'There was little or no street crime in Brixton at the time. As kids we were able to play in the streets – I am sure that the Majors did not, because that was a working-class practice only. If anyone was unfortunate enough to be knocked over when we were playing in the streets, you could bet your bottom dollar that he would be knocked over by a car that was designed and built in Britain. It would be an Austin or a Morris Oxford or, if he was very lucky, or perhaps unlucky, he could be knocked over by a Jowett Javelin. How I longed to be run over by a Jowett Javelin. There were no beggars in the streets of Brixton in the 1950s, there was no one pushing drugs. Truancy was almost inconceivable and anyone who did it found that the school inspectors or the educational welfare officers would soon come round to talk with his parents. To own a television in Brixton in the 1950s was a big deal … must have been the golden age of basics for the Prime Minister. I was lucky – I saw every match that Chelsea played in the great year of 1954-55.'

Chapter 8

THE GLORIOUS FINALE:
NUTS IN THE BOARDROOM
(April 1955)

'Fifty years without a single honour. Nothing but ridicule from chalk-faced comedians. An eternally-empty sideboard. That's the Chelsea FC history for you.'

These words, from *Soccer Star* magazine in April 1955, reflected the nation's shock that Ted Drake's team were in with a great chance of winning the championship crown as the season drew towards its climax. The magazine writers may have been getting excited, but most Chelsea fans regarded the situation with philosophical caution. There was still time for the dream to be shattered. Still time for mercurial Chelsea to mess things up. On the first Saturday in April, for example, the team would have to do without key men Frank Blunstone and Ken Armstrong. Both had been called up for England duty against Scotland at Wembley, the latter for his senior debut. The pair subsequently played their part in a 7-2 win for Walter Winterbottom's side, with Wolves' Dennis Wilshaw bagging four goals.

The absence of Blunstone at Tottenham was again covered by the unorthodox Brabrook-Willemse partnership in attack. To deputise for Armstrong, Drake sprang another surprise, calling up Alan Dicks, a twenty-year-old wing-half who hadn't made a first team appearance in eighteen months. Londoner Dicks had played for London schoolboys and embarked on a career in accountancy when Chelsea signed him from under the noses of Millwall. The deciding factor was a £250 signing-on fee which Dicks later claimed he never received. He hoped to follow in the footsteps of older brother Ronnie, who went on to play more than 500 games for Middlesbrough, but Alan only enjoyed rare chances in Chelsea's first team. With points so vital at White Hart Lane on 2nd April, this call-up represented a nerve-wracking day for young Dicks.

Chelsea went to White Hart Lane determined not to give an inch and their muscular approach paid off in an eventful game which left their old rivals from North London infuriated. The *Tottenham and Edmonton Weekly Herald* reflected the fury of the home fans: 'Outclassed in the finer arts of the game, Chelsea became the toughest, roughest and crudest team to visit White Hart Lane for many a season … never have the fans seen so many fouls committed in one game … unpenalised body-checking, booting the ball into the crowd and ungentlemanly conduct. There should have been more than just Bentley's booking on 85 minutes [Chelsea's skipper had committed four fouls in two minutes and about a dozen infringements in all]. In the space of 30 seconds Willemse knocked [Peter] Baker on to the running track and upended [John] Gavin. He repeatedly raised the "V" sign in front of the directors box after being jeered for booting the ball into the crowd. He twice kicked the ball away when Blanchflower was about to take a free-kick. Chelsea may have ceased to be the butts of the vaudeville comedians, but they'll never get another funny line anywhere if they go on playing like this.'

Strong stuff, and it wasn't just the animated Tottenham press who condemned Chelsea's display that afternoon. *The Times* recorded: 'Chelsea had a propensity for playing the man rather than the ball, which made their performance unconvincing. The finer points of the game were practiced by [Spurs].' Such comment did not concern Chelsea, who were jubilant at their 4-2 victory. Twice the home side's Ted Duquemin had struck with fine goals, but on both occasions the Blues bounced back with scrambled equalisers and then netted twice more to take two precious points. The last four goals came in a fast and furious fourteen-minute spell midway through the second half. The last of all, cementing the win, was a Peter Sillett penalty given for a contentious Baker handball.

Chelsea had exploited Tottenham's fragile confidence and taken advantage of the lenience of referee Pollard. The home side felt hard done by, but this was typical of their recent luck, for they were going through hard times. Their manager, Arthur Rowe, was suffering from a debilitating illness, thought to be partly due to the stress of his job. Spurs' goalkeeper that day – Ron Reynolds – would later reveal that Rowe was a pleasant man who hated being ruthless, and as results deteriorated in 1955 he crumbled under the pressure. A few weeks after the Chelsea defeat, Rowe stood down. The crisis at White Hart Lane, recalled Reynolds, was such that there were even rows between the team's two 'quiet men', Alf Ramsey and Bill Nicholson.

Inside-right Johnny McNichol considered the victory at Tottenham to be the result that turned Chelsea from mere contenders into champions-elect. Not only did they come from behind twice, but they achieved the win without key men. He recalled that Stan Willemse was spat at by the home crowd when he ran out of the tunnel that day, and for Chelsea to go on to win had given the team a huge lift.

With the nation digesting the news of Prime Minister Winston Churchill's resignation on 5th April, Easter approached with Chelsea enjoying a four-point lead at the top of the League. Traditionally they did not fare well over this holiday period – they had gone seven Easters without a win. Both 1955 holiday games were at home this year, so those two games could be make-or-break as far as Chelsea's title hopes were concerned. First up was the visit of Sheffield United on Good Friday. That game offered a great opportunity to widen the gap, for Wolves were without a fixture. Just under 51,000 turned up, only to endure a hugely disappointing encounter. Perhaps due to over-anxiety and the need to preserve energy for the following day's 'four pointer', Chelsea looked sluggish and uncomfortable. Jack Cross shot the Blades ahead in the first half and it took a late rescue-act from the quicksilver Eric Parsons to save a point.

The top of the table, following those Good Friday fixtures, 8th April, was as follows:

	P	W	D	L	F	A	Pts
Chelsea	38	18	11	9	76	55	47
Wolves	35	16	10	9	79	57	42
Portsmouth	35	17	18	10	64	48	42
Manchester C	36	16	19	11	69	58	41
Sunderland	37	12	17	8	56	50	41

It was clear a huge improvement would be needed just twenty-four hours later for the big clash with second-placed Wolves at Stamford Bridge. And had it not been for Parsons' timely intervention against Sheffield United, the task would have seemed even bigger. Parsons was already a big crowd favourite, but his 75th-minute equaliser elevated his popularity further. Fans loved his crouching, scampering runs down the right flank, nicknamed him 'The Rabbit', and roared their delight every time he skinned a full-back. Born in Worthing, thirty-one year old Parsons signed professional with West Ham at nineteen and spent more than seven years with the Second Division club, making 145 League appearances. He had moved to Chelsea and been hit by a series of injuries by the time Ted Drake arrived as manager, but the new boss boosted his self-confidence and gave him a new lease of life. Parsons was blessed with tremendous pace and plenty of skill and would surely have won full England honours had Tom Finney and Stan Matthews not been around at the same time.

For the massive test against Wolves, Drake was able to recall Seamus O'Connell in place of rookie Peter Brabrook and was relieved to find no injuries from the Sheffield United game the previous day. Wolves had the advantage of not having played for a week, spending several days relaxing by the sea at Ramsgate, supervised by trainer Joe Gardner. They left their hotel in Kent on the morning of the match and travelled by rail into London. Despite the disappointing Good Friday game, everything about the Wolves fixture seemed upbeat. The atmosphere was more positive and the fans in fine voice, apparently determined to help their heroes as much as they could. With a five-point advantage at the top, surely a win today would end Wolves' hopes altogether. It was a situation almost too good to even contemplate. The Stamford Bridge gates were closed forty-five minutes before kick-off with more than 75,000 already crammed inside. Outside the ground, mounted police turned disappointed late-comers away. Ten minutes before the teams came out, thousands of fans already inside climbed over the rails to sit on the greyhound track, with police and officials powerless to get them back. But as a threat of a pitch invasion seemed unlikely, the police were not unduly alarmed and allowed them to stay where they were.

When play began, Chelsea surprised their critics by looking the fresher of the two sides. Roared forward by their biggest crowd of the season, they went agonisingly close through Parsons' drive, Bentley's flying header, and a thirty-five-yard rocket from Sillett, all of which brought agile saves from veteran keeper Bert Williams. Just before the break it was still goalless when Parsons cut the ball back to give Bentley the sort of chance he normally gobbled up, but the skipper somehow scuffed the chance and Wolves breathed again. The visitors' lively winger, Roy Swinbourne, was by this time limping with a knee injury and Wolves were beginning to look ill at ease.

After the interval, Chelsea goalkeeper Chick Thomson's first serious action was to block a long-range free-kick from Johnny Hancocks. O'Connell missed another chance for Chelsea and it was beginning to look like a goalless draw was on the cards when the game's great drama suddenly unfolded. Williams fisted out a cross to the feet of O'Connell, who fired the ball towards the top corner. It beat Williams' dive, but behind him Billy Wright punched the ball over the bar.

Following Sillett's successful penalty, Wolves threw everything forward. Little Hancocks switched to centre-forward, beat his marker Stan Wicks, and fired a shot from twenty yards which smashed against a post. The rebound was hacked clear by Derek Saunders. Moments later Hancocks was obstructed inside the area. All eleven Chelsea players were behind the ball as Dennis Wilshaw – an England hero seven days earlier – flicked the indirect free-kick to Hancocks, whose shot swerved wide.

With an estimated 3,000 more people attempting to squeeze into the packed ground after the gates were opened at half-time, the noise was by now deafening. Repeated assaults by Wolves kept Chelsea hearts in mouths. The final whistle sparked the inevitable pitch invasion. Last man off was the dejected figure of Williams, who had played a blinder to no avail, and scowled angrily as the crowd applauded him off.

Sillett's penalty winner cast in stone his legendary status at Chelsea. With a huge fourteen-stone frame and deceptively laid-back approach, Sillett often transferred play from one end to the other with massive punts upfield, and could display great accuracy in dead-ball situations. He first came to prominence at home-town club Southampton and the cash-strapped Saints reluctantly accepted a fee of £13,000 to sell him in mid-1953. Sillett had by now established himself in the Chelsea first team and had been joined at the club by younger brother John. Peter was even being touted as worthy of an England call-up.

On Easter Sunday, Chelsea players relaxed with their families in the knowledge that now the title really was within their grasp. Much of the rest of the country felt that Chelsea were about to become champions by default. The over-riding feeling was that Wolves had thrown it away. Stan Cullis's men had gone into serious decline since being ousted from the FA Cup by Sunderland on 12th March. Before that tie, they had won four games in a row, scoring nineteen goals. Afterwards, they failed to win any of their next four, scoring just three. Wolves' away form in particular had gone to pieces. It was beginning to look like fourth-placed Portsmouth might pose the most serious threat to Chelsea's title ambitions – even though they had just gone down 1-3 at West Brom.

Following the Easter Saturday games, Chelsea would still need to win all three remaining games to be sure of the title, but only if Wolves or Portsmouth won all six of theirs, which was unlikely. Indeed, Chelsea's forty-nine points might already be enough (as in fact it was).

Sadly, there were no newspapers to cover Chelsea's finest hour against Wolves. The strike also meant reduced coverage on the Monday of Ruth Ellis, a nightclub hostess from North London, who had shot her lover, the well-known racing driver David Blakely, outside a Hampstead pub. Ellis would become the last woman to be hanged in Britain.

On Easter Monday, Wolves kept their slim title hopes alive by grabbing their first win in over five weeks. Emergency centre-forward Ron Flowers snatched an 87th-minute winner in their home game with Aston Villa. But twenty-four hours later they slumped to a 2-4 defeat in the return at Villa Park, thus giving more cause for celebration in south-west London. After games on Tuesday, 12th April, the table read:

	P	W	D	L	F	A	Pts
Chelsea	39	19	11	9	77	55	49
Wolves	38	17	10	11	82	62	44
Portsmouth	37	17	9	11	67	53	43
Manchester C	38	17	9	12	71	60	43
Arsenal	38	17	8	13	64	54	42

Having put paid to the Wolves threat, Chelsea now had to take on the other main challengers, Portsmouth, at a Fratton Park that had been something of a hoodoo venue in the past. The League placings meant that avoiding defeat would be tantamount to a victory. Goalkeeper Thomson recalls sharing a railway carriage with Drake and trainer Jack Oxberry on the way down to Portsmouth: 'They were talking about just what was needed from each game to win the title. They had really started to believe that the title was ours and it was fascinating listening to them going through all the permutations and what they thought our rivals would get out of their remaining fixtures … it had never entered my head before, but it suddenly dawned on me that I may not have played enough games to qualify for a medal if we won, so I interrupted them and asked if they knew how many games you needed to qualify. "You're playing it today," said Ted, to my relief.'

Thomson made a couple of fine saves as the Fratton Park showdown stayed goalless. Near the end, Les Stubbs joyfully drove the ball home, only for offside to be called. To this day the players believe it was a legitimate goal. Stubbs was only playing because O'Connell was on duty for Bishop Auckland in the FA Amateur Cup final at Wembley. The point earned was just what was needed, even though Wolves kept alive their faint hopes by beating Arsenal 3-1 at Molineux. Chelsea were four points ahead of Wolves with two games left, Cullis's men having one in hand.

Then, on Wednesday 20th April, Wolves crumbled 0-3 at Manchester City, a result which all but ended their challenge. The picture was now becoming clearer. The title could be clinched on the season's penultimate Saturday if Chelsea beat already-relegated Sheffield Wednesday and Portsmouth dropped a point at Cardiff. This was the table, after games on Wednesday, 20th April. Four clubs were still in the hunt.

	P	W	D	L	F	A	Pts
Chelsea	40	19	12	9	77	55	50
Wolves	40	18	10	12	85	66	46
Portsmouth	38	17	10	11	67	53	44
Manchester C	39	17	10	12	72	61	44

The national newspaper strike was settled on 21st April, which meant that the Sheffield Wednesday crunch match received a full and proper build-up – and a somewhat surprised football nation prepared to herald the arrival of new League champions. Desmond Hackett of the *Daily Express* apologised humbly for having claimed emphatically in February that Chelsea would *not* win the League. The days of Chelsea being the clown princes of football, the court jesters of sport, are over, he now admitted.

It was generally assumed that already-doomed Wednesday would be easy meat for Chelsea, but some observers noted that they had been playing with a new freedom recently, a freedom which had seen them win their last two games. Owls' manager Eric Taylor insisted the bottom had not dropped out of their world, claiming his was a young side with a good future. The 51,421 who converged on Stamford Bridge on Saturday, 23rd April raised the season's home aggregate attendance to over one million – a new club record. Attendances had fluctuated widely, from a low of 30,000 to see Burnley, up to 75,000-plus to watch Wolves. Supporter G Burgin of Notting Hill registered the millionth click of the turnstiles and was presented with a season ticket for the following campaign.

Perhaps inevitably, the game was no footballing classic. As against Blackpool and Sheffield United, Chelsea hardly had the poise of champions, looking tense and unable to express themselves – paralysed no doubt by the importance of the occasion. There was bad news in the early stages when the loudspeakers revealed that Portsmouth had gone ahead at Cardiff through Peter Harris. After that, there was little to excite the spectators until the vital Chelsea breakthrough arrived – Parsons' header converting a Blunstone cross midway through the first half. Not even that goal could ignite the game as a spectacle, and many fans continued to twitch nervously. Shortly after half-time, visiting keeper David McIntosh was carried off with a back injury, having fallen awkwardly after a hefty barge from Bentley. McIntosh was taken to hospital in some pain and full-back Norman Curtis took over the green jersey.

Midway through the second half came the goal that finally settled the nerves and made the points safe. Jackie Sewell – back helping his Owls defence – was harshly judged to have handled a shot by Saunders. Most observers thought the ball had hit his shoulder, and a muddy mark on his shirt seemed to confirm this. Makeshift keeper Curtis had no chance with Sillett's penalty, slotted carefully into the corner – a cool kick as opposed to the bombshell he had unleashed from the spot against Wolves. Five minutes later a Parsons' shot looked to be covered by Curtis, only for the ball to slide through his hands for a soft goal. None of the three strikes were picture goals and the match itself was not one for the purists – *The Times* went so far as to describe it as 'a misery in terms of quality' – but the result was all that mattered. Now, all that was needed was for Portsmouth to be denied victory at Cardiff.

The crowd, although informed earlier of Cardiff's equaliser against Portsmouth, invaded the Stamford Bridge pitch at the final whistle, oblivious to the final score at Ninian Park. The Chelsea players were engulfed under an avalanche of well-wishers. Backs were slapped, hands pumped and hair ruffled, but eventually the players reached the sanctuary of the dressing room. Chances to celebrate, to celebrate anything, had been all too rare at Chelsea, and this opportunity wasn't going to be wasted by the fans. The mayhem continued long after the players had disappeared, the mass of spectators waiting as patiently as they could for some kind of confirmation that the championship was won. The news took nearly fifteen minutes to arrive, but it was worth waiting for. The loudspeakers burst into crackly life, announcing that Portsmouth had indeed only drawn. That meant Chelsea were the new champions. Supporters of all ages danced like lunatics on the damaged turf and demanded the reappearance of the manager and players.

Soon the heroes, one by one, appeared up in the Main Stand by the directors box. Some wore tatty tracksuits with towels round their necks, but manager Drake looked smart in his double-breasted blazer. Skipper Bentley grabbed the hastily-installed microphone, and surviving film footage recorded his exact words: 'Well, on behalf of the boys, I'd like to thank you. There's no need to tell you how pleased we are to win the championship, but we're pleased for you because you've been behind us in other years and more so this year. So, from the bottom of our hearts, I say thank you very much.' [Huge roar].

Next to take the microphone was Ted Drake: 'This is the happiest moment of my life,' he said, the hint of a choke in his voice. He paused to swallow hard and looked close to tears. Another huge cheer erupted, and he continued: 'I was asked, would we win the cup, and I thought we might, but I thought we had a great chance of winning the championship even better.' Chairman Mears and defender Wicks could now be seen close to Drake's shoulder, and Mears appeared to wipe a tear away with a handkerchief as the hordes sang and danced below.

These were wonderful, unforgettable moments for the fans who witnessed them. With hindsight, they seem all the more poignant because this was pretty much all there was in terms of celebration. In modern times, newly-crowned champions milk their success with a series of well-organised receptions, parades, and all manner of celebratory events.

For Chelsea's supporters and players in 1955 it was very different. Apart from these brief speeches from the directors box there was precious little for the public to enjoy. The trophy would be paraded briefly around the ground before the following season kicked off, but that, folks, was your lot. In the years since, players and fans have reflected sadly on what a shame it was that Chelsea's finest hour was allowed to pass with such little fanfare, and how the atmosphere quickly went flat. For many who had waited so long for this moment, there was a real sense of anticlimax. Part of the problem, perhaps, was that the Easter game with Wolves had provided the real crunch, and the excitement of that day simply couldn't compete with beating forlorn Sheffield Wednesday.

Bentley said recently: 'I remember the day we won the league as if it was yesterday. We didn't really celebrate and just had some nuts in the boardroom with our wives. Ted said a few words, I said a few words and then we all went home. Stan [Willemse] went down for an evening at Brighton races, so he tells me. Everyone asks what we got for winning the league, but Stan nearly had the police after him. We were invited to a tailors and could either have a suit or an overcoat as a reward. Stan ordered both and when Ted got the bill he wasn't impressed!'

Blunstone feels it was just coincidence that Chelsea won the League in the club's jubilee season. He said nobody had mentioned the anniversary until the end of the season, and could recall no celebrations to mark the occasion: 'After the Sheffield Wednesday game we went into the directors' box ... but there was no trophy at the ground or anything and we certainly never ran round the pitch.' Goalkeeper Thomson described the championship celebrations as 'almost completely flat' and said the players had to wait weeks for their medals. Some sort of ceremony would have been nice, he felt, and it was a pity the fans didn't see any trophies presented at Stamford Bridge. Thomson would later win the FA Cup with Nottingham Forest and see for himself the uplifting effect of a proper celebration. That Wembley win made him realise what the Stamford Bridge die-hards had missed out on. The League medals were eventually distributed in the boardroom over a meal by chairman Joe Mears, he recalled. Thomson added that he had created a bigger celebration himself when out with footballing mates Dave Ewing (Manchester City) and Doug Winton (Burnley) later in the summer.

Willemse recalled fondly the events after the final whistle against Sheffield Wednesday, but after that it was very 'low key' and he caught his usual train home and went to Brighton track to see his dogs running. McNichol remembered looking down at all the thousands on the pitch, but said this was short-lived and that five of the players simply went to their favourite café around the corner for a cup of tea and some chips. As a Scotsman, he still finds it hard to understand such low-key celebrations: 'It was a cuppa, a chip butty and an early night!'

Lewis said recently it was clear that absolutely no thought and little preparation had been put in, even though the club knew how close they were to clinching the biggest prize in its history. Having viewed the old footage of the day he was amused and incredulous over the scruffy tracksuits being worn in the directors box. The other players received special championship suits, but as an amateur he was not allowed to accept one. Instead he was later awarded an illuminated scroll in a frame. As his wife frowned on memorabilia in the Lewis living room, that scroll had hung for fifty years in the toilet!

Stubbs recalled the end-of-season club dinner at which Chairman Mears stood to toast the players one by one. He would bang his knife on the side of his glass, stand up, call one of the names out, drain his glass and then sit back down again. This went on until he couldn't stand any more and – allegedly – passed out completely.

After turning their backs on the celebrating fans massed on the pitch, the players filed into the gymnasium to be interviewed by the BBC. Drake, Bentley and Parsons all appeared live on Sports Report. Shortly afterwards the players, their wives and close friends were invited into the directors' private room where a beaming Drake read out telegrams that had been pouring in. The Saturday night football editions of the London evening papers were brought in and proclaimed the new champions, convincing any disbelievers that Chelsea really had won something.

Once the dust had settled, *The Times* could be relied upon to wax lyrical on the season's climax: 'The taxi driver, the artist, the chimney sweep and the actor, who have rubbed shoulders at Stamford Bridge can at last ride roughshod over the jibes aimed for so long at dear old Chelsea. They are no longer unpredictable. The whiskered Chelsea director bent under top hat and weighed down by heavy watch chains, made infamous in cartoon by the pen of Mr Tom Webster, is decently buried for the moment. Even the miniature figure of the footballer supporting the weather vane over the stand – some say it is a replica of Hilsdon, years ago the centreforward of Chelsea and England – now has a new, purposeful look. Perhaps all this transformation can be traced to the moment three years ago when, under new management, that affectionate old emblem of the Pensioner disappeared from the Chelsea crest. With him went the dillydallying Chelsea of old, a Chelsea with a reputation for friendly and gentle, sometimes doddering artistry, but a Chelsea who exasperated by their failure to achieve results.'

Another football writer, Brian Glanville, pointed out the irony of how, down the years, Chelsea had spent relatively high amounts on players, but when they finally did gain their solitary championship it was with a team put together at minimal cost. In the *Daily Express*, Tommy Lawton, a former Chelsea favourite now with Arsenal, reviewed the season and seemed reluctant to praise his former club's achievement, preferring to heap praise on the likes of Portsmouth and Manchester City for their attractive attacking styles.

Meanwhile, Johnny McNichol blamed the newspaper strike for the fact that 'so little is known about Chelsea's championship win'. He reckoned the reports that were printed after the strike ended were rarely complimentary and he could not fathom what had rubbed the press up the wrong way about Chelsea. Wolves and Manchester United, he recalled, were treated in a far more complimentary fashion when they won their titles in the mid-1950s.

Chelsea had won the championship with one game to play:

	P	W	D	L	F	A	Pts
Chelsea	41	20	12	9	80	55	52
Wolves	41	19	10	12	87	67	48
Manchester C	41	18	10	13	76	67	46
Sunderland	41	14	18	9	61	54	46
Portsmouth	39	17	11	11	68	54	45

Four days later the new champions saw the other side of the football coin when a full-strength team travelled the short distance to non-league Hayes to fulfil a midweek friendly commitment, which they won 8-0 at the humble Church Road ground. The curtain came down on this historic season with a trip to Old Trafford for the final League game, the result of which was academic. Manchester United's players sportingly formed a guard of honour to welcome Chelsea on to the field, as the band played 'See the Conquering Heroes Come'. Willemse reflected later that it had been a fantastic honour that such a good side had given them such respect, but he was pleased when the whistle went for the start of the game 'so we could go back to hating them again!'

Chelsea lost 1-2 at Old Trafford and so finished the season as the lowest points-scoring champions since the First Division was expanded to twenty-two clubs. But as Wolves went down 2-3 at Cardiff on the same day, Chelsea still retained a four-point cushion at the top. Portsmouth also lost their final match, on 1st May, 2-5 at Sheffield United, which condemned them to third place. Chelsea's reserves lifted the Football

Combination title, their 'A' team won the Metropolitan League, and their juniors won the South East Counties League – an astonishing clean sweep at Stamford Bridge, the like of which will surely never be repeated again.

There was no immediate rest for the conquering heroes, who had to set off on the now-traditional end-of-season tour in early May for games with Shamrock Rovers of Dublin (2-3), French clubs Lens (1-1) and Rouen (4-2), and a Dutch national side (2-2). Incidentally, the match programme for the Lens game has become a real collector's item. It attracted bids of more than £1,500 when one was placed on the e-Bay auction website in 2004.

The weary trio of Sillett, Bentley and Blunstone had even more footballing commitments, for they were selected for a three-match England tour, starting directly after Chelsea's return from the Continent. 'It's a great life to be a footballer of note in the modern world,' reflected *The Times*. 'He spans the globe by aircraft, making his bow in all the huge stadiums of the Continents. More than that, he is an ambassador of his country, on and off the field, where both his skill and his demeanour are critically appraised.' With Sillett gaining his first full cap, England went down 0-1 to France in Paris, drew 1-1 with Spain in a bad-tempered affair in Madrid (Bentley the scorer) and lost 1-3 to Portugal in Porto (Bentley on target again). A few days later Willemse collected his boots and headed off with England 'B' to take part in a 0-2 defeat by Switzerland in Basle. Now, at last, with June fast approaching, the new League champions could finally put their feet up.

Chapter 9

How the Mighty Fell

(Post-1955)

There was definitely something unreal about Chelsea FC becoming Champions of England in April 1955.

Maybe it was because the club had never won anything previously, or their modest points tally, but Chelsea's reputation as a team of spoilers, hard men with little finesse, seems to have persuaded some people that Chelsea did not actually win the title, it was more a case of the more complete Wolves outfit carelessly tossing it away.

All this was just sour grapes to the Chelsea supporters and players – although most of them would ruefully agree the triumph had been a 'one-off' that might never be repeated. Chelsea had given everything, out-reaching themselves in one supreme, sustained effort. They had beaten Wolves twice and amassed more points than anyone else, so it was surely churlish to suggest they were not worthy champions. It was ironic that after years of being labelled under-achievers, Chelsea were now being told they'd over-achieved, and the success wouldn't last.

Perhaps Drake knew deep down that his men were unlikely to repeat their League heroics, for he made no secret of his insistence that Chelsea would go all out to win the FA Cup when the new season got under way. Before 1955-56 began, however, there was a side issue that needed sorting out – the little matter of the new European Cup.

Earlier in 1955 the French sports paper *L'Equipe* and its editor Gabriel Hanot had championed the cause of a European-wide club competition. Hanot, together with colleague Jacques Ferran, designed a blueprint for a challenge tournament to be played on Wednesday evenings under floodlights. The rules did not, in its inaugural season, stipulate that participating teams had to be champions of their country. Representatives of sixteen countries convened in early April and the *L'Equipe* proposal was unanimously approved. Having won the English championship, Chelsea were asked to come and join the party. But it was an invitation they would be pressured into not accepting.

The recent friendlies between Wolves and Honved, and Chelsea and Red Banner, had attracted huge interest and there was considerable enthusiasm for the idea of the tournament – but that enthusiasm was not shared by Alan Hardaker, the powerful secretary of the Football League. Hardaker did not want English clubs involved in this half-baked idea and put pressure on Chelsea chairman Joe Mears – also a serving League official – to turn down the invitation to take part. For their part, Scottish club Hibernian happily accepted their nomination – Hibs had finished fifth, which incensed Scottish champions Aberdeen – and thereby became the first British club to participate in European competition. They subsequently reached the semi-finals.

In the years since 1955, the dictatorial Hardaker has been severely chastised for his negative attitude towards European football, and accused of xenophobia. Brian Glanville says Hardaker 'bullied' Chelsea into not competing and alleged the League's supremo had said some 'monstrous' things about foreigners. Fortunately for the development of English football, Matt Busby and Manchester United refused to cave in to pressure the following year, and United became England's first representatives in the flourishing new competition. Hardaker exacted revenge on Busby in 1958: he coerced the FA into blocking United's acceptance of a wild-card invitation to play in Europe, which had been a goodwill gesture following the Munich disaster.

So, with no European football to whet the appetite, Chelsea began the defence of their League title in August 1955 with the same side that had won it. This was a worry for forward-thinking Chelsea supporters, for this was clearly an ageing team likely to get worse before it got better. Key men like Bentley, Willemse, Parsons and Armstrong were all thirty, not forgetting Harris who was nearer forty. Only Brabrook, Smith and possibly Tindall looked ready to step up from the younger reserve ranks to take over from the fading stars.

The first game of the new season was at home to Bolton, preceded by a short parade around the ground with the championship trophy. The party atmosphere soon soured as the reigning champs were beaten 0-2 by Bill Ridding's men. Chelsea bounced back four days later with a 3-1 triumph at Huddersfield, but this false dawn was followed by a nightmarish spell of seven games without victory. It dropped Chelsea to 21st place in the division. The low-point was a 1-5 home thrashing by Portsmouth, an embarrassment that led to drastic team changes, most of which were short-term measures only.

The previously out-of-favour Bobby Smith was hastily recalled and hit four goals in three games, but again the improvement was only temporary. By Christmas Chelsea were stuck in mid-table with just nine wins from twenty-two games – hardly the form expected of defending champions. It was a case of 'normal service is resumed' as far as most fans were concerned. Having tasted League success, they now fancied a crack at the Cup, anyway.

Drake wasn't panicking, however, and there were few signs of new faces being introduced. An exception was Ron Tindall's goalscoring debut against West Brom. Drake liked what he saw in Tindall and, as a result, felt able to sell Bobby Smith – the Yorkshireman moving across London to Spurs, for whom he scored on his Christmas Eve debut and went on to achieve cult status.

The players who won the title may not have celebrated wildly back in April, but at Christmas 1955 they certainly tried to make up for it. Having travelled to Cardiff by train on Christmas Day for a Boxing Day fixture at Ninian Park, a bunch of senior players secretly hatched a plan to have crates of brown ale spirited up to one of their hotel rooms. The plan was to wait until Ted Drake had gone to bed, then have a party – even though the next day's kick-off time was 11.30 in the morning. It was well past midnight when the racket woke Drake. He stormed in and read the riot act. Stan Willemse recalled this as one of the very few occasions he ever saw the boss lose his temper. The guilty players apparently escaped further punishment. The team held Cardiff 1-1 and then beat them 2-1 in the return in London twenty-four hours later.

When attention turned to the FA Cup in early 1956, Chelsea wrote themselves into the record books when their fourth-round tie with Burnley went to no fewer than *five* games, three of them featuring extra-time. After nine hours of deadlock, Chelsea progressed to the fifth round by winning the fourth replay 2-0. The players were publicly lauded by Drake for showing grit and determination. It had been an extraordinary record-breaking episode of five matches in eighteen days, often in dreadful wintry conditions, enough to tax the fittest of players. But it begged the question, why couldn't they show the same bite in the League?

The Burnley saga remained an all-time FA Cup record until 1971-72, when Alvechurch and Oxford City needed six games before a winner emerged. The exertions took a serious physical toll on Chelsea players: nor was there any chance to pause for breath, because the fifth round tie at Everton was scheduled for just three days later. To their credit, Chelsea fought like tigers at Goodison but went down 0-1. Drake said he had really fancied his men for the Cup this year and was distressed by events, but full of praise for his brave heroes. Asked why these same players couldn't halt the club's simultaneous slide down the League, he simply said: 'I just can't put my finger on what's wrong.'

The slide that dumped the reigning champions to the fringe of relegation by mid-April 1956 was blamed by Drake on his own, and the team's, ambitions to win the FA Cup. He told the *Sunday Express*. 'The [team] were on a determined special effort this year. We made one mistake. We never allowed for anything like that Burnley cup marathon. Up to that cup defeat by Everton we had a fine prospect of finishing in the League talent money. Then came defeat at Everton – a bitter disappointment to the boys. The reaction was both physical and mental. The side slumped. It was a tough job. Up to [then] we were a real fighting side. The enthusiasm and snap – qualities that win games – vanished.'

The League plight reached a critical point in mid-April when Chelsea found themselves facing Everton at Stamford Bridge without a win in their last nine League games. Two points against Cliff Britton's men would ensure safety. Thankfully the misery of recent weeks was blown away as the boys in blue rose to the occasion and thrashed Everton 6-1, Bentley snapping a hat-trick. The supporters had given the occasion a big thumbs-down, though, for a pitifully low 13,825 turned out, one of the lowest Saturday gates in the club's history. Earlier in the season, even fewer (less than 9,000) had attended the game with Charlton – a far cry from the 75,000 who had witnessed the Wolves match less than twelve months earlier.

On the same day that Chelsea had tackled Charlton before a sparsely-populated Stamford Bridge, Portsmouth and Newcastle were permitted to stage the first League match under floodlights. Fratton Park suffered a power cut in the dressing rooms and offices, forcing the players to change in darkness, but the game went ahead and afterwards everyone present hailed floodlit League football a winner. It meant the end was in sight for poorly-attended midweek afternoon games.

Chelsea finished 1955-56 in a hugely disappointing sixteenth place. How are the mighty fallen. As Drake surveyed the wreckage, he vowed to begin dismantling the side that had won the championship. Slowly but surely this is what he did, introducing youngsters to replace established stars and prompting the press to dub them Drake's Ducklings. Within six months of this pivotal decision, six of his title-winning squad had moved on. Stan Willemse went to Leyton Orient, John Harris to Chester, Roy Bentley to Fulham, Stan Wicks quit through injury, Eric Parsons joined Brentford, and Seamus O'Connell was released. A year or two later Ken Armstrong retired, Chick Thomson joined Nottingham Forest, and Jim Lewis and Johnny McNichol moved on. Frank Blunstone and Peter Sillett would be the only regulars from the championship side who were still around five years on.

Youngsters Brabrook, Tindall, Mortimore, Greaves, Bridges, Tambling, Bonetti, Harris and Venables would prove the most successful of the so-called Drake's Ducklings. Many others were plunged into the side, but quickly pulled out again. Transfer-market purchases were few and far between, but they included England goalkeeper Reg Matthews for £20,000 from Coventry, half-back Stan Crowther from Manchester United for £10,000 and Celtic's thirty-two-year-old centre-half Bobby Evans for £12.500. Drake was praised in some quarters for his bravery in entrusting Chelsea's future to youth, but chided in others for ditching the experienced men far too quickly. The process meant results were mixed throughout the late 1950s and the finishing place of sixteenth in 1955-56 was followed by thirteenth, eleventh, fourteenth, eighteenth, and twelfth in subsequent years. Few would argue that even these small mercies were achieved only by one factor – the goals of the young prodigy Jimmy Greaves.

If ever one player could have fended off relegation almost single-handedly, and saved a declining side from instant relegation, it was Greaves. Given his debut as a raw seventeen-year-old at the start of 1957-58, this supreme goal-poacher became an instant sensation. From day one his goal output was phenomenal. Inevitably, it was not long before the young superstar became frustrated with the mediocrity around him. According to Matt Allen's biography *Jimmy Greaves*, he was frustrated by the club's slack attitude. The board seemed satisfied with mid-table medi-ocrity and behind the scenes apathy ran rampant. Defeats were laughed off and the atmosphere in the Chelsea dressing room was often more jovial than in the winners' next door. On top of this, the powers-that-be at Stamford Bridge had made it clear they disapproved of Greaves get-ting married so young. This seemed bizarre to him, as he felt he was set-tling down and maturing.

These years of transition and unrest at the Bridge are remembered distinctly by John Major, the future Prime Minster, who was by then in his teens: 'I can still smell the cheroot smoke and roasted peanuts of a sunny Easter afternoon when they beat Everton 6-2 and Jimmy Greaves scored five goals. Such a result had rarity value, quite apart from the odours of the day.'

Another fan with clear memories of these troubled times in Chelsea's history is Richard Posner: 'My abiding memory of being a Chelsea sup-porter during this period was one of general gloom and despondency, relieved occasionally by one outstanding performance.

'I was out of the country when Jimmy Greaves made his debut and was still away on holiday for the game against Wolves which we won 5-1, when Jimmy really made his name, running rings round Wolves and the England captain, Billy Wright. I always knew one day Jimmy would leave

– it was just too good to be true for Chelsea to have a player like him. I remember coming down to breakfast one morning before school, grabbing the *Daily Express* – a broadsheet in those days – turning immediately to the back page and seeing in big bold letters the headline I had always dreaded: 'Greaves Wants a Transfer.' That was it, the game was up, life would never be the same again. It took quite a while before he finally left so I think the fans were ready for it by then, but this didn't really soften the blow and we all knew we had lost a really special talent.

'Frank Blunstone was always my personal favourite, and a big crowd favourite too. He was an outside-left who ran fast with his head down, beating all and sundry on his way to the opponents' goal-line. And let no-one forget that the original Cheeky Chappie was a great footballer called Terry Venables. He came into the Chelsea side as a right-half, then when Johnny Hollins came into the team, was moved to inside-left. A right-half playing at inside-left? Was this madness? The fans were amazed, whatever next? My abiding memory of Tel is him crouching behind the referee as play developed and then coming out of hiding to nick the ball off an opposing player. It happened, it really did. Peter Brabrook was a great player who provided a devastating partnership with Greaves on the right-wing. He looked like a gypsy, and played like one, all tricks and selling dummies.'

One of Richard's favourite 1950s Chelsea anecdotes involves a holiday in Israel with his family: 'After two weeks of tedious touring, we finally arrived at the seaside resort of Herzlia where at last I could buy a ball and play football on the beach. My father joined me and we went into the sea to play headers. After a while I heard the sound of loud Cockney voices, young lads larkin' about in the water. I turn round to see what this strange phenomenon was ... remember I'm a 13-year-old Chelsea fanatic, Chelsea are my life, and there, standing only yards from me in the water, are Terry Venables, Peter Brabrook, Allan Harris and the rest of the Chelsea team. They are on an end-of-season tour. I am speechless. My father is not; he'll talk to anyone, even the gods. He goes up to Harris: "So what do you all think of Jimmy Greaves leaving, then?" he asks. "Well", Allan replies, "Y'know, if it's what 'e wants, more money an' 'at, good luck to 'im, y'know." My father is not impressed and walks away, leaving me standing there in the water with my heroes. I don't know how it happened but pretty soon I'm having a kickabout with the entire Chelsea first team on the beach at Herzlia. Can this be happening?'

Back to the harsh and chilly reality of Stamford Bridge, Posner recalls: 'From 1955 until we went down, it was all pretty dreadful, despite many of the championship side still being in the team. The typical match was a 0-0 draw with Manchester City on a cold November Saturday – they all seemed like that! I remember a home game against the Busby Babes in 1956 or 1957: They were all over us, different class, and this was only a couple of years after the championship. We always seemed to lose away to the Boltons and Burnleys of this world 0-2, and the home games were a complete lottery, for you'd never know which Chelsea would turn up. I remember the game to celebrate the installation of floodlights at Stamford Bridge. It was 19th March 1957 – my ninth birthday – and what a present. This was the most exciting thing since we had central heating installed at home. A night game against foreigners! Before floodlighting, games started at 2.15 in the winter so that they would finish before it got dark.'

Chelsea's reputation as a music-hall joke seemed to be gaining momentum again in the late 1950s, despite the title success. In less than five years Chelsea had gone from League champions to a team that in attitude and outlook resembled little more than a pub side. Drake summed up the club (perhaps for all time?) when he described his lads as 'Good players never getting anywhere'. He had become increasingly pre-occupied with assembling a young side modelled on the Busby Babes at Old Trafford. However Drake's so-called Ducklings were a rag-tag mob of raw kids, whereas United's babes were a carefully created blend of youth and experience. Lambs were being sent to the slaughter at the Bridge, several having leapfrogged the reserves straight into the first team, when patently not ready. Drake struggled throughout the late 1950s to find a decent defensive formation and, worryingly, was increasingly absent from the training ground in midweek due to an old back complaint which confined him to his office.

Greaves netted as astonishing tally of 124 goals in only four League seasons (157 games) while part of this inconsistent side, and before long the inevitable happened and he was sold. He bid an emotional farewell to the Stamford Bridge faithful in the spring of 1961 by scoring four against Nottingham Forest. Referring to the malaise at the club at that time, Greaves reflected sadly: 'I feared that if I stayed in the Chelsea atmosphere too long I might lose my fine cutting edge as a player'. He then had a distinctly short and unhappy spell in Milan and within months was back in London, frustratingly choosing Spurs above Chelsea as his new stamping ground.

Shortly before he left Chelsea, Greaves and his teammates were reportedly offered a 'bung' to throw a match. Greaves says the cash incentive came from two Nottingham Forest players, whose side were battling relegation in the 1960-61 season. In his autobiography, Greaves says: 'Before our game against Forest, captain Peter Sillett called a team meeting and said: "Two Forest lads have approached me. They're worried about relegation and are desperate for points. They have £500 to be shared among us if we throw the game and let them win".' (The average annual wage in the UK in 1961 was around £1,000). Greaves, who scored as the two teams drew 1-1, never discovered the names of the Forest pair and said he had not come across anything like it in football before or since.

Jimmy Greaves' much-lamented departure was followed by a further slump in results, and after a sequence of just two wins from the first eleven games of 1961-62, Ted Drake, the fallen hero, was sacked. The writing had been on the wall for some time. Eight months earlier Chelsea had been humiliated at home in the FA Cup by little Crewe, an outfit who a year beforehand had been annihilated 2-13 by Tottenham. Chelsea were 21st in the table when Drake departed, and looking strong candidates for relegation. The young and inexperienced coach Tommy Docherty was appointed manager, but not even his enthusiasm and fresh ideas could save Chelsea from the drop. Relegation was confirmed in April 1962, exactly seven years after the club's finest hour. The decline had been slow but inexorable.

So what became of the boys of '55?

Goalkeeper Chick Thomson moved to Nottingham Forest in August 1957, where he had four relatively successful years, appearing in the 1959 FA Cup final victory over Luton Town.

His fellow custodian Bill Robertson remained on Chelsea's books until September 1960, but slipped behind Reg Matthews in the first-team pecking order. He had two seasons at Leyton Orient before moving to Dover in May 1963. He died in Tadworth, Surrey, in June 1973, aged just forty-four.

England 'B' international Stan Willemse was sold to Leyton Orient for £4,500 in June 1956. He had two seasons at Brisbane Road before quitting, initially to become a publican. He is now retired in Hove.

Defender John Harris moved to Chester in July 1956, where he played and managed the Sealand Road side before taking charge of Sheffield United in April 1959. He managed the Blades until December 1973 and was their longest-serving post-War boss, winning promotion twice. He died in July 1988.

Full-back Peter Sillett remained a Stamford Bridge stalwart until 1962, by which time a broken leg had ended his top-flight career. He had won three full England caps and been a non-playing squad member at the 1958 World Cup finals in Sweden. In July 1962 he joined non-league

Guildford, then Ashford and Hastings, and also scouted for his brother John, the Hereford manager, with whom he had played at Chelsea. He died in Ashford, aged sixty-five, in March 1998.

Right-half Ken Armstrong passed the 400-appearance mark to set a club record before retiring from the English game in 1957. He emigrated to New Zealand to seek new challenges after receiving medical advice that a warmer climate would benefit a chest complaint. In 1971 he became New Zealand's oldest National League player at almost forty-seven. He coached Mount Wellington to success and the team featured his sons Ron and Brian, who both won caps for New Zealand. He held various national coaching roles before his death in 1984. His ashes were scattered over the Stamford Bridge pitch.

Wing-half Alan Dicks moved to Southend United in November 1958, where he played around 100 times in four years before going into coaching. He assisted Jimmy Hill at Coventry before spending thirteen largely successful years (October 1967 to September 1980) in charge of Bristol City. He had spells in Greece, Cyprus and Qatar, followed by a year at Fulham, rejoining Jimmy Hill, who was chairman at Craven Cottage. A stint in the USA was followed by his return to the Bristol area.

Centre-half Stan Wicks blossomed into a player of England international potential after Chelsea won the title, but his career was cut short by a knee injury in his eighty-first Division One game in September 1956, against Sheffield Wednesday, and he never played again. He ran the family carpet business in Reading and died in February 1983 of cancer.

Centre-half Ron Greenwood left for Fulham during the title-winning season but played enough games to qualify for a medal. As widely expected, he move into coaching and became assistant manager at Arsenal in November 1958 before landing the top job at West Ham in April 1961. A long and happy association with the Hammers saw him become temporary manager of England in August 1977 and full-time boss four months later. He resigned after the 1982 World Cup having led his country in fifty-four internationals. England remained unbeaten in the 1982 tournament, although eliminated, and Greenwood's team also won the British championship three times under his control. He was made an MBE and won other merit awards from football writers and the PFA. In retirement he settled at Hove on the south coast.

Left-half Derek Saunders played on until the 1958-59 season, making more than 200 appearances in all, before taking up a coaching role at Stamford Bridge. He later moved on to become soccer coach and groundsman at Westminster School and also worked in adult education circles in London.

England 'B' international Eric Parsons left Chelsea for Brentford in November 1956, and made well over 100 appearances for the Griffin Park side before having a spell at Dover. He ran a grocery store and then started a cigarette vending business, before retiring to his seaside flat in Worthing. He is a talented bowls player and added the English national titles to numerous victories at local level in Sussex.

Winger Frank Blunstone played on until 1964, passing the 300-game mark, until an Achilles tendon injury suffered on an end-of-season tour ended his playing career. Earlier on, a broken leg had interrupted his progress and without these injuries he might well have added to his five England caps. Blunstone beat John Bond, among others, for the managerial vacancy at Brentford in December 1969. He won promotion with The Bees and later assisted Tommy Docherty at Manchester United and Derby County. After coaching at Sheffield Wednesday he retired to his native Crewe area in 1991.

Winger Peter Brabrook emerged after the title win as one of London's star performers, playing 270 times for Chelsea and earning three England caps. In October 1962 West Ham boss Ron Greenwood reunited himself with the player when swooping to buy Brabrook for £35,000. At Upton Park he became a cog in one of the country's most attractive attacking sides. His Football League career ended in 1971 at Orient, whom he had joined in July 1968. He turned out for Romford and managed Billericay.

Inside-forward Johnny McNichol lost his regular place in the Chelsea side due to the emergence of starlet Jimmy Greaves, and it seems his days became numbered after he took over a newsagent's shop, which manager Drake felt interfered with his football. He moved on to Crystal Palace in March 1958, where he made around 200 appearances, not quitting the Football League until into his late thirties. He player-managed at non-league level with Tunbridge Wells and then worked in Palace's fund-raising department for eleven years. He did similar work at Brighton before retiring in 1992. Like Parsons, he enjoys retirement from a sea-view home on the south coast.

England amateur international Seamus O'Connell only made a handful of appearances after the title was won, preferring to concentrate on his family's cattle farming business, while making the odd appearance for home town Carlisle and Crook Town as an amateur. He quit football in 1958, aged twenty-eight, and eventually settled permanently in Spain. He made a big impact in a short time at Chelsea, but has been a notable absentee from the periodic re-unions of the 'Boys of '55'.

England amateur star Jim Lewis had three further seasons at Chelsea, usually filling in for injured colleagues, before returning in May 1958 to

Walthamstow Avenue, where he played until 1966. He retired from the game with a super set of statistics to his name. For Chelsea, Walthamstow Avenue, England Amateurs and the GB Olympic team, he totalled a remarkable 506 goals in 673 games.

Bustling inside-forward Les Stubbs left Chelsea in November 1958, having totted up thirty-four goals in 112 League games, to rejoin Southend United in a five-figure deal that also included Alan Dicks. After just twenty-two games in his second spell at Roots Hall, Stubbs became involved in a pay dispute and quit to join the fire brigade. After a year with Bedford Town he left to concentrate on his work as a physical training officer with the fire service. He has lived in the small Essex town of Great Wakering all his life and played for the local team into his fifties.

The most influential player of the title-winning group was centre-forward and skipper Roy Bentley. After seven successive seasons as top scorer, he left Chelsea in September 1956 for neighbours Fulham – but not in entirely happy circumstances. He had been promised a coaching role at the Bridge and was shocked to be released: 'I couldn't believe it,' he recalls. 'I had been promised from my early days that I'd go on the coaching staff and never leave Chelsea. But it wasn't Ted Drake's fault – he said if he'd had his way I would have stayed.' At thirty-two, Bentley still had plenty to offer and made around 150 appearances for Fulham before two seasons with Queen's Park Rangers in the early 1960s.

Bentley says: 'I went to Fulham and QPR and learned about management and coaching. Alec Stock was fantastic to learn from, he was superb at man management and a marvellous man himself. He said to me: "You were a better player than me, so I can't tell you what to do. But what I can tell you is what *not* to do! Money was short and the club couldn't afford new balls so Alec painted some old ones white.' In 1963 Bentley became manager of Reading and held the role for six years before three seasons in charge at Swansea. He later returned to Reading as club secretary. 'I found it very difficult to retire,' he recalls. 'Football is a seven-days-a-week thing and when you go into management it becomes 10-days-a-week.'

And what of the boss? After leaving Chelsea to make way for the brash young Tommy Docherty in 1961, Ted Drake stayed in football in various capacities at Fulham, where his son Bobby was on the playing staff. Drake was invited to become a member of the first Pools Panel, created in January 1963, alongside Tom Finney, Tommy Lawton, George Young and Arthur Ellis. Alzheimer's disease eventually took its toll and Drake died aged 82 in May 1995.

GUIDE TO SEASONAL SUMMARIES

Col 1: Match number (for league fixtures); Round (for cup-ties).
e.g. 4R means 'Fourth round replay.'

Col 2: Date of the fixture and whether Home (H), Away (A), or Neutral (N).

Col 3: Opposition.

Col 4: Attendances. Home gates appear in roman; Away gates in *italics*.
Figures in **bold** indicate the largest and smallest gates, at home and away.
Average home and away attendances appear after the final league match.

Col 5: Respective league positions of Chelsea and opponents after the game.
Chelsea's position appears on the top line in roman.
Their opponents' position appears on the second line in *italics*.
For cup-ties, the division and position of opponents is provided.
e.g. 2:12 means the opposition are twelfth in Division 2.

Col 6: The top line shows the result: W(in), D(raw), or L(ose).
The second line shows Chelsea's cumulative points total.

Col 7: The match score, Chelsea's given first.
Scores in **bold** show Chelsea's biggest league win and heaviest defeat.

Col 8: The half-time score, Chelsea's given first.

Col 9: The top line shows Chelsea's scorers and times of goals in roman.
The second line shows opponents' scorers and times of goals in *italics*.
A 'p' after the time of a goal denotes a penalty; 'og' an own-goal.
The third line gives the name of the match referee.

Team line-ups: Chelsea line-ups appear on top line, irrespective of whether
they are home or away. Opposition teams are on the second line in *italics*.
Players of either side who are sent off are marked !
Chelsea players making their league debuts are displayed in **bold**.

LEAGUE DIVISION 1 — Manager: Ted Drake — SEASON 1954-55

Column headings: No | Date | Att | Pos | Pt | F-A | H-T | Scorers, Times, and Referees | 1 2 3 4 5 6 7 8 9 10 11

---

1. A LEICESTER — 21/8 — Att 38,941 — D 1-1 (H-T 0-0) — Pt 1

Scorers: Bentley 70 / Griffiths 55. Ref: A Ellis

	1	2	3	4	5	6	7	8	9	10	11
Chelsea	Robertson	Sillett	Willemse	Harris	Greenwood	Saunders	Parsons	McNichol	Bentley	Stubbs	Blunstone
Leicester	*Anderson*	*Milburn*	*Jackson*	*Baldwin*	*Gillies*	*Russell*	*Griffiths*	*Morris*	*Rowley*	*Hines*	*Froggatt*

Norman Bullock's side are back in the top flight after 15 years. Both sides miss chances galore. Blunstone goes off hurt in the first half. A free-kick finds Mal Griffiths, who fires home. Bentley nets an equaliser in a breakaway raid. McNichol hits a late chance straight at John Anderson.

---

2. H BURNLEY — 23/8 — Att 30,239 — W 1-0 (H-T 0-0) — Pt 3

Scorers: Parsons 67. Ref: L.Howarth

	1	2	3	4	5	6	7	8	9	10	11
Chelsea	Robertson	Sillett	Willemse	Harris	Greenwood	Saunders	Parsons	McNichol	Smith	Stubbs	Lewis
Burnley	*McDonald*	*Aird*	*Mather*	*Adamson*	*Cummings*	*Seith*	*Gray*	*McIlroy*	*Holden*	*Shannon*	*Pilkington*

Bentley and Blunstone are out injured and a drab start has the fans slow-handclapping. McNichol goes close with long-range shots, and Stubbs misses a sitter. Lewis's cross finds Parsons, who runs the ball in. Bill Holden thunders a drive against the bar with the final kick of the match.

---

3. H BOLTON — 28/8 — Att 52,756 — W 3-2 (H-T 1-2) — Pos 4 — Pt 5

Scorers: Bentley 44, Lewis 57, Ball 76 (og) / Parry 7, Moir 20. Ref: G Pankhurst

	1	2	3	4	5	6	7	8	9	10	11
Chelsea	Robertson	Harris	Willemse	Armstrong	Greenwood	Saunders	Parsons	McNichol	Bentley	Stubbs	Lewis
Bolton	*Hanson*	*Ball*	*Banks*	*Wheeler*	*Barrass*	*Edwards*	*Holden*	*Moir*	*Lofthouse*	*Hassall*	*Parry*

Bill Ridding's men forge ahead as Ray Parry heads through Robertson's hands and then Willie Moir nets a rebound off the bar. Bentley heads in a Lewis cross to begin the comeback. Lewis hits a post and nets the rebound. After heavy pressure, Lewis's corner deflects in off John Ball.

---

4. A BURNLEY — 31/8 — Att 28,472 — D 1-1 (H-T 0-0) — Pos 2 — Pt 6

Scorers: Bentley 75 / Pilkington 88. Ref: L Howarth

	1	2	3	4	5	6	7	8	9	10	11
Chelsea	Robertson	Harris	Willemse	Armstrong	Greenwood	Saunders	Parsons	McNichol	Bentley	Stubbs	Lewis
Burnley	*McDonald*	*Aird*	*Mather*	*Adamson*	*Cummings*	*Shannon*	*Gray*	*McIlroy*	*Holden*	*McKay*	*Pilkington*

On the hottest day of the year, Bentley goes close with a header and then has another effort disallowed. Eventually he lobs home from a Stubbs pass. Chelsea claim Bill Holden and Brian Pilkington 'sandwiched' Robertson before the equaliser is knocked in, but the referee is unmoved.

---

5. H CARDIFF — 4/9 — Att 42,688 — D 1-1 (H-T 0-0) — Pos 6 — Pt 7

Scorers: Lewis 84 / Tiddy 75. Ref: N Taylor

	1	2	3	4	5	6	7	8	9	10	11
Chelsea	Robertson	Harris	Willemse	Armstrong	Greenwood	Saunders	Parsons	McNichol	Bentley	Stubbs	Lewis
Cardiff	*Howells*	*Stitfall*	*Sherwood*	*Harrington*	*Montgomery*	*Baker*	*Tiddy*	*Williams*	*Grant*	*Nugent*	*Edwards*

Cliff Nugent injures his shoulder to make life easier for the home defence, in which Greenwood is impeccable. Colin Baker stabs the ball to Mick Tiddy, whose hopeful 20-yarder beats a late-reacting keeper. Chelsea's blushes are spared as Lewis heads home Armstrong's fine cross.

---

6. H PRESTON — 6/9 — Att 31,947 — L 0-1 (H-T 0-0) — Pos 8 — Pt 7

Scorers: Foster 68. Ref: R Leafe

	1	2	3	4	5	6	7	8	9	10	11
Chelsea	Robertson	Harris	Willemse	Armstrong	Greenwood	Saunders	Parsons	McNichol	Bentley	Edwards	Lewis
Preston	*Thompson*	*Cunningham*	*Walton*	*Docherty*	*Marston*	*Forbes*	*Finney*	*Foster*	*Wayman*	*Baxter*	*Morrison*

Tonight's winners will go top of the table. Chelsea batter the visitors during the first half to no avail. Preston soak up the pressure and then take the lead as Tom Finney's skimmed cross is sidefooted past Robertson by Bobby Foster. It's a great start to the season for new boss Frank Hill.

---

7. A MANCHESTER C — 11/9 — Att 36,230 — D 1-1 (H-T 0-0) — Pos 10 — Pt 8

Scorers: Bentley 65 / Paul 64. Ref: R Coultas

	1	2	3	4	5	6	7	8	9	10	11
Chelsea	Robertson	Harris	Willemse	Armstrong	Greenwood	Saunders	Parsons	McNichol	Bentley	Stubbs	Lewis
Man City	*Trautmann*	*Meadows*	*Little*	*Barnes*	*Ewing*	*Paul*	*Fagan*	*McAdams*	*Revie*	*Hart*	*Clarke*

Les McDowall's men exert heavy pressure after the break and the ref misses a blatant handball in the area. He spots a similar offence further out, however, by Armstrong and the free-kick is lashed in by skipper Roy Paul. Spirited Chelsea hit straight back as Bentley seizes on an error.

---

8. A PRESTON — 15/9 — Att 27,749 — W 2-1 (H-T 1-0) — Pos 8 — Pt 10

Scorers: McNichol 18, Parsons 46 / Wayman 75. Ref: R Leafe

	1	2	3	4	5	6	7	8	9	10	11
Chelsea	Robertson	Harris	Willemse	Armstrong	Greenwood	Saunders	Parsons	McNichol	Bentley	Stubbs	Lewis
Preston	*Thompson*	*Cunningham*	*Walton*	*Docherty*	*Marston*	*Forbes*	*Finney*	*Foster*	*Wayman*	*Baxter*	*Morrison*

A Lewis cross is nodded down by Bentley for McNichol to shoot home. The purposeful Parsons gets his reward just after the break. Charlie Wayman pulls one back. Willie Forbes is injured and hobbles around as a passenger on the left wing, but twice nearly levels close to the end.

---

9. H EVERTON — 18/9 — Att 59,199 — L 0-2 (H-T 0-2) — Pos 10 — Pt 10

Scorers: Parker 31, Eglington 34. Ref: F Read

	1	2	3	4	5	6	7	8	9	10	11
Chelsea	Robertson	Harris	Willemse	Armstrong	Greenwood	Saunders	Parsons	McNichol	Bentley	Stubbs	Lewis
Everton	*O'Neill*	*Moore*	*Donovan*	*Farrell*	*Jones*	*Lello*	*McNamara*	*Fielding*	*Hickson*	*Parker*	*Eglington*

Cliff Britton's men punish Chelsea for missing four glorious early chances. Parsons hits a post then fluffs a header, and Stubbs fires straight at the keeper. Dave Hickson heads on a clearance and Tommy Eglington pounces for the first. Hickson then sets up John Parker for the clincher.

---

10. A SHEFFIELD UTD — 20/9 — Att 14,127 — W 2-1 (H-T 1-1) — Pos 6 — Pt 12

Scorers: Lewis 2, Stubbs 80 / Shaw G 35. Ref: H Broadhurst

	1	2	3	4	5	6	7	8	9	10	11
Chelsea	Robertson	Harris	Willemse	Armstrong	Greenwood	Saunders	Parsons	McNichol	Bentley	Stubbs	Lewis
Sheffield Utd	*Hodgkinson*	*Furniss*	*Shaw G*	*Hoyland*	*Shaw J*	*Rawson*	*Ringstead*	*Hagan*	*Hawksworth*	*Luke*	*Grainger*

Lewis nets an early goal after Fred Furniss blocks a Parsons effort. Graham Shaw levels after a hectic spell of Blades attacking. Ten minutes from time Bentley sets up Stubbs for a winner. The home side feel hard done by, but Chelsea's defence did well to withstand all the pressure.

Match 11 — NEWCASTLE (A), 25/9
Pos 4 · W 3-1 (HT 3-0) · Att 45,659 · 11 · 14
Scorers: Bentley 6, 19, McNichol 17 — Milburn 67
Ref: J Williams

Pos	1	2	3	4	5	6	7	8	9	10	11
Chelsea	Robertson	Harris	Willemse	Armstrong	Greenwood	Saunders	Parsons	McNichol	Bentley	Smith	Lewis
Newcastle	*Simpson*	*Cowell*	*McMichael*	*Scoular*	*Brennan*	*Crowe*	*Milburn*	*Davies*	*White*	*Broadis*	*Mitchell*

A fine display sinks Duggie Livingstone's men. Bentley links with Parsons for the first, then Lewis hits a second, then Bentley nets Willemse's cross. Ronnie Simpson collides with a post and Jimmy Scoular has a spell in goal. Jackie Milburn bags a consolation.

Match 12 — WEST BROM (H), 2/10
Pos 4 · D 3-3 (HT 1-1) · Att 67,440 · 1 · 15
Scorers: Bentley 11, Parsons 62, Lewis 65 — Allen 20, Lee 80, Millard 88
Ref: H Webb

Pos	1	2	3	4	5	6	7	8	9	10	11
Chelsea	Robertson	Harris	Willemse	Armstrong	Greenwood	Saunders	Parsons	McNichol	Bentley	Smith	Lewis
West Brom	*Saunders*	*Rickaby*	*Millard*	*Dudley*	*Dugdale*	*Kennedy*	*Griffin*	*Ryan*	*Allen*	*Williams*	*Lee*

Cup-holders and league leaders WBA attract a lock-out crowd. Bentley finds an empty net for his 100th Chelsea goal. Ronnie Allen levels with a soft goal. Parsons and a Lewis' rising drive make it 3-1. Back come Albion via George Lee, then Len Millard levels with a long-range rocket.

Match 13 — HUDDERSFIELD (A), 9/10
Pos 9 · L 0-1 (HT 0-1) · Att 29,556 · 11 · 15
Scorers: Cavanagh 31
Ref: B Griffiths

Pos	1	2	3	4	5	6	7	8	9	10	11
Chelsea	Robertson	Harris	Willemse	Armstrong	Greenwood	Saunders	Parsons	McNichol	Bentley	Stubbs	Lewis
Huddersfield	*Wheeler*	*Staniforth*	*Kelly*	*McGarry*	*Taylor*	*Quested*	*Burrell*	*Watson*	*Glazzard*	*Cavanagh*	*Metcalfe*

Tom Cavanagh's firm drive gives Andy Beattie's side a deserved lead. They should have scored more, with Jim Glazzard spurning two great chances. Chelsea abandon their short-passing game near the end and directness nearly pays off. Bentley has a late strike disallowed for offside.

Match 14 — MANCHESTER U (H), 16/10
Pos 11 · L 5-6 (HT 2-3) · Att 55,996 · 1 · 15
Scorers: O'Con' 20, 67, 76, Lewis 35, Arm' 61 — Viol' 15, 41, 57, Tay' 38, 48, Blan' 63
Ref: C Kingston

Pos	1	2	3	4	5	6	7	8	9	10	11
Chelsea	Robertson	Harris	Willemse	Armstrong	Greenwood	Saunders	Parsons	McNichol	Bentley	O'Connell	Lewis
Manchester U	*Wood*	*Foulkes*	*Byrne*	*Gibson*	*Chilton*	*Edwards*	*Berry*	*Blanchflower*	*Taylor*	*Viollet*	*Rowley*

A truly astonishing game. O'Connell bags a debut hat-trick but ends up on the losing side. Eight goals during a 32-minute passage of play. The last 25 minutes features frenzied Chelsea attacking and they go agonisingly close to clawing back a three-goal deficit. Fabulous entertainment.

Match 15 — BLACKPOOL (A), 23/10
Pos 12 · L 0-1 (HT 0-0) · Att 19,694 · 20 · 15
Scorers: Fenton 51p
Ref: J Gardner

Pos	1	2	3	4	5	6	7	8	9	10	11
Chelsea	Robertson	Harris	Willemse	Armstrong	Greenwood	Saunders	Parsons	McNichol	Bentley	O'Connell	Lewis
Blackpool	*Farm*	*Shimwell*	*Garrett*	*Fenton*	*Johnston*	*Kelly*	*Matthews*	*Taylor*	*Mortensen*	*Brown*	*Perry*

Chelsea's short-passing game is overcome by a more direct approach. Joe Smith has called up his 'old guard' and they inspire the struggling home side. Stan Mortensen is brought down for the decisive penalty as he chases an Ernie Taylor pass. Chelsea slip into the table's lower half.

Match 16 — CHARLTON (H), 30/10
Pos 12 · L 1-2 (HT 0-2) · Att 54,113 · 8 · 15
Scorers: Parsons 89 — Firmani 10, 15p
Ref: K Collinge

Pos	1	2	3	4	5	6	7	8	9	10	11
Chelsea	Robertson	Harris	Willemse	Armstrong	Greenwood	Saunders	Parsons	Smith	Bentley	O'Connell	Lewis
Charlton	*Bartram*	*Campbell*	*Townsend*	*Hewie*	*Ufton*	*Hammond*	*Hurst*	*O'Linn*	*Ayre*	*Firmani*	*Kiernan*

Eddie Firmani heads in after Willemse's blunder and the full-back then handles the penalty. Firmani rams home the penalty. Chances are missed after the break, then Sam Bartram is finally beaten near the end. A fourth defeat in a row and no home wins since August.

Match 17 — SUNDERLAND (A), 6/11
Pos 12 · D 3-3 (HT 2-2) · Att 42,416 · 2 · 16
Scorers: McNichol 19, 24, Stubbs 68 — Snell 8, Shackleton 18, Purdon 69
Ref: J Williams

Pos	1	2	3	4	5	6	7	8	9	10	11
Chelsea	Robertson	Harris	Willemse	Armstrong	**Wicks**	Saunders	Parsons	McNichol	Bentley	Stubbs	Lewis
Sunderland	*Fraser*	*Headley*	*McDonald*	*Anderson*	*Daniel*	*Snell*	*Bingham*	*Shackleton*	*Purdon*	*Chisholm*	*Elliott*

Wicks makes an impressive debut on a greasy pitch, but can't prevent Bill Murray's men cruising into a two-goal lead. A superb fight-back sees McNichol grab two and Stubbs nets a cracking drive past a diving Bill Fraser. South African Ted Purdon brings the Rokerites level again.

Match 18 — TOTTENHAM (H), 13/11
Pos 12 · W 2-1 (HT 2-0) · Att 52,961 · 21 · 18
Scorers: Lewis 7, Bentley 8 — Gavin 81
Ref: J Pollard

Pos	1	2	3	4	5	6	7	8	9	10	11
Chelsea	Robertson	Harris	Willemse	Armstrong	**Wicks**	Saunders	Parsons	McNichol	Bentley	Stubbs	Lewis
Tottenham	*Reynolds*	*Ramsey*	*Withers*	*Nicholson*	*Clarke*	*Marchi*	*Gavin*	*Baily*	*Dunmore*	*Brooks*	*Robb*

Harry Clarke kicks an effort off the line but Lewis pounces to score. A minute later Bentley is left unmarked and converts a low Parsons cross. Bill Nicholson brings down Parsons in the second half but the penalty is missed. John Gavin grabs a late goal and Chelsea are left hanging on.

Match 19 — SHEFFIELD WED (A), 20/11
Pos 12 · D 1-1 (HT 1-1) · Att 25,913 · 22 · 19
Scorers: McNichol 83 — Sewell 29
Ref: W Ling

Pos	1	2	3	4	5	6	7	8	9	10	11
Chelsea	Robertson	Harris	Willemse	Armstrong	Wicks	Saunders	Parsons	McNichol	Bentley	Stubbs	Lewis
Sheffield Wed	*Ryalls*	*Conwell*	*Curtis*	*Gannon*	*O'Donnell*	*Shaw*	*Finney*	*Quixall*	*Sewell*	*Froggatt*	*Marriott*

Jackie Sewell takes a Jack Marriott pass and streaks clear to net a low drive. Robertson plays well and prevents a real hammering. Willemse is injured and becomes a limping passenger on the wing. In a rare attack Blunstone hits a post. McNichol saves the day with a lob in off the post.

Match 20 — PORTSMOUTH (H), 27/11
Pos 11 · W 4-1 (HT 2-1) · Att 40,358 · 6 · 21
Scorers: Blunstone 28, Bentley 31, McNich' 75, [Stubbs 85] — Henderson 34
Ref: R Smith

Pos	1	2	3	4	5	6	7	8	9	10	11
Chelsea	Robertson	Harris	Willemse	Armstrong	Greenwood	Saunders	Parsons	McNichol	Bentley	Stubbs	Blunstone
Portsmouth	*Uprichard*	*McGhee*	*Mansell*	*Phillips*	*Gunter*	*Pickett*	*Harris*	*Gordon*	*Henderson*	*Barnard*	*Dale*

Eddie Lever's side cancel out Blunstone's breakthrough goal with an overhead kick from Jackie Henderson. Bentley restores the lead, falling as he fires home. McNichol beats Tom McGhee and sprints clear to net. A fine win is capped by Stubbs' amazing drive from around 40 yards.

Match 21 — WOLVERHAMPTON (A), 4/12
Pos 8 · W 4-3 (HT 1-1) · Att 32,095 · 1 · 23
Scorers: McNich' 16, Bentley 52, 87, Stubbs 86 — Broad't 17, Swin' 76, Hancock 83p
Ref: J Malcolm

Pos	1	2	3	4	5	6	7	8	9	10	11
Chelsea	Robertson	Harris	Willemse	Armstrong	Greenwood	Saunders	Parsons	McNichol	Bentley	Stubbs	Blunstone
Wolverhampton	*Williams*	*Stuart*	*Shorthouse*	*Slater*	*Wright*	*Flowers*	*Hancock*	*Broadbent*	*Swinbourne*	*Wilshaw*	*Smith*

McNichol cracks in a beauty from Parsons' cross. Stan Cullis's reigning champs level from Roy Swinbourne's cross. Bentley restores the lead and the final 15 minutes sees four goals and a shock result in the Molineux mud. Bentley secures the win, breaking clear to beat Bert Williams.

LEAGUE DIVISION 1

Manager: Ted Drake — SEASON 1954-55

No	V	Opponents	Date	1	2	3	4	5	6	7	8	9	10	11	Scorers, Times, and Referees	H-T	F-A	Res	Pt	Pos	Att
22	H	ASTON VILLA	11/12	Robertson	Harris	Willemse	Armstrong	Greenwood	Saunders	Parsons	McNichol	Bentley	Stubbs	Blunstone	Parsons 15, McNichol 60, 77, [Bentley 81] — Ref: C Curtis	1-0	4-0	W	25	4 / 19	36,162
				Jones	*Lynn*	*Aldis*	*Birch*	*Moss*	*Crowe*	*Lockhart*	*Dixon*	*Pace*	*Follan*	*McParland*							
23	H	LEICESTER	18/12	Robertson	Harris	Willemse	Armstrong	Greenwood	Saunders	Parsons	McNichol	Bentley	Stubbs	Blunstone	Parsons 13, Milburn/Froggatt 28 (og), Graver 82 [McNichol 78] — Ref: A Ellis	2-0	3-1	W	27	4 / 21	33,215
				Anderson	*Milburn*	*Jackson*	*Baldwin*	*Froggatt*	*Russell*	*Griffiths*	*Worthington*	*Rowley*	*Hogg*	*Graver*							
24	A	ARSENAL	25/12	Robertson	Harris	Willemse	Armstrong	Greenwood	Saunders	Parsons	McNichol	Bentley	Stubbs	Blunstone	Lawton 36 — Ref: B Buckle	0-1	0-1	L	27	5 / 19	47,178
				Kelsey	*Barnes*	*Evans*	*Goring*	*Fotheringham*	*Bowen*	*Clapton*	*Tapscott*	*Lawton*	*Lishman*	*Haverty*							
25	H	ARSENAL	27/12	Robertson	Sillett	Willemse	Armstrong	Wicks	Saunders	Parsons	McNichol	Bentley	O'Connell	Blunstone	O'Connell 80, Tapscott 8 — Ref: B Buckle	0-1	1-1	D	28	5 / 19	45,922
				Kelsey	*Barnes*	*Evans*	*Goring*	*Fotheringham*	*Bowen*	*Clapton*	*Tapscott*	*Lawton*	*Lishman*	*Haverty*							
26	A	BOLTON	1/1	Hanson	Sillett	Willemse	Armstrong	Wicks	Saunders	Parsons	O'Connell	Bentley	Stubbs	Blunstone	O'Connell 4, Bent'y 41, 57, Sillett 78p, Barras 73, 80p [Higgins 81 (og)] — Ref: G Pankhurst	2-0	5-2	W	30	4 / 16	51,988
					Ball	*Bingley*	*Wheeler*	*Higgins*	*Edwards*	*Pilling*	*Hennin*	*Hassall*	*Barrass*	*Parry*							
27	H	MANCHESTER C	22/1	Thomson	Sillett	Willemse	Armstrong	Wicks	Saunders	Parsons	McNichol	Bentley	Stubbs	Blunstone	Hayes 48, Clarke 79 — Ref: F Coultas	0-0	0-2	L	30	6 / 8	34,160
				Trautmann	*Meadows*	*Little*	*Barnes*	*Ewing*	*Paul*	*Fagan*	*Hayes*	*Revie*	*Hart*	*Clarke*							
28	A	EVERTON	5/2	Thomson	Sillett	Willemse	Armstrong	Wicks	Saunders	Parsons	McNichol	Bentley	Stubbs	Blunstone	Bentley 73, McNamara 8 — Ref: F Reed	0-1	1-1	D	31	6 / 7	50,558
				O'Neill	*Moore*	*Donovan*	*Farrell*	*Jones*	*Lello*	*McNamara*	*Fielding*	*Hickson*	*Parker*	*Eglington*							
29	H	NEWCASTLE	12/2	Thomson	Sillett	Willemse	Armstrong	Wicks	Saunders	Parsons	McNichol	Bentley	Stubbs	Blunstone	Bentley 22, 60, 63, McNichol 59, Keeble 75, 81, Milburn 88 [Stubbs 76] — Ref: J Clough	1-0	4-3	W	33	5 / 11	50,867
				Simpson	*Woollard*	*Batty*	*Scoular*	*Stokoe*	*Crowe*	*Milburn*	*Davies*	*Keeble*	*Hannah*	*Mitchell*							
30	H	HUDDERSFIELD	26/2	Thomson	Sillett	Willemse	Armstrong	Wicks	Saunders	Parsons	McNichol	Bentley	Stubbs	Blunstone	Pars'ns 55, Blunstone 56, Bent'y 75, Burrell 44 [Stubbs 76] — Ref: M Griffiths	0-1	4-1	W	35	3 / 11	35,746
				Wheeler	*Staniforth*	*Kelly*	*McGarry*	*Taylor*	*Quested*	*Burrell*	*Watson*	*Glazzard*	*Frear*	*Metcalfe*							
31	A	ASTON VILLA	5/3	Thomson	Sillett	Willemse	Armstrong	Wicks	Saunders	Parsons	McNichol	Bentley	Stubbs	Blunstone	McNichol 32, Parsons 64, Walsh 25, 34, McParland 82 — Ref: C Curtis	1-2	2-3	L	35	5 / 11	24,822
				Jones	*Lynn*	*Aldis*	*Baxter*	*Martin*	*Crowe*	*Southren*	*Gibson*	*Walsh*	*Dixon*	*McParland*							

Match reports

22. Chelsea's bogey side are shown no mercy. Parsons' curling free-kick is helped in by Keith Jones. Eric Houghton's men are sunk as McNichol nets after a Parsons solo run. Blunstone sets up McNichol and Bentley to end in style. Red Banner's squad (Hungary) watch from the stands.

23. After Parsons opener, Stan Milburn and Jack Froggatt lunge at the same loose ball and it flies into their own net. The referee confirms it will be recorded as a joint effort! Bentley has a penalty saved, but McNichol fires a third. Debutant Andy Graver rounds Greenwood to pull one back.

24. Tom Whittaker's injury-hit Gunners give Danny Clapton a debut, and despite going down to ten men, show no Christmas Day cheer towards Chelsea. The off-form Blues are sunk by 35-year-old Tommy Lawton, who shows his old magic with a turn and shot from Wally Barnes' pass.

25. Derek Tapscott puts the Gunners ahead early and they repel all the Blues' first-half efforts. On 53 minutes Bentley sees his penalty pushed over the bar by Jack Kelsey – the fifth successive spot-kick the team has missed. Relief as Bentley's headed pass sets up O'Connell for an equaliser.

26. Bill Ridding's men, missing five regulars, have Harold Hassall carried off. O'Connell's header and scrambled Bentley goal sets Chelsea up. A trip on O'Connell allows Sillett to crack home a penalty and end the recent jinx. Stand-in forward Malcolm Barrass pulls back two late goals.

27. After inactivity due to bad weather, Chelsea catch a cold. Roy Paul feeds Roy Clarke, whose cross is glanced in by Joe Hayes. Clarke collects Fionan Fagan's cross, eludes Wicks and fires another. City's innovative deep-lying No 9 system (the 'Revie plan') has worked its magic again.

28. Cliff Britton's men surge ahead through Tony McNamara's shot. John Parker has an effort cleared off the line by Willemse, while Stubbs hits the bar for Chelsea. With Dave Hickson off for treatment, Bentley levels with a flying header, pushed onto a post and in by diving Jim O'Neill.

29. Ronnie Simpson fumbles a Parsons shot and Bentley heads home. Three goals in four minutes stun Duggie Livingstone's outfit. Vic Keeble brings the Geordies back into contention, poaching two quick goals then Jackie Milburn buries a fine effort after a corner. The Blues hang on.

30. Gerald Burrell forces in James Watson's cross. Chelsea hit back via Parsons after his first shot rebounds off Jack Wheeler. After Stubbs' error, Blunstone nips in to lob a second. Wheeler's goal-kick is returned from 45 yards high into the net by Bentley. Unhappy Wheeler gifts a fourth.

31. David Walsh bags a solo goal before McNichol finishes off some good work by Bentley. Tommy Southren sets up Walsh again. Parsons nets a Bentley centre to level, but Peter McParland bags a soft winner after Thomson palms a cross straight to him. Chelsea slip out of the top three.

No	H/A	Date	Opponent	Pos	Pl	Res	FT	HT	Pts	Att
32	A	9/3	WEST BROM	19	3	W	4-2	0-2	37	7,764
33	H	12/3	BLACKPOOL	20	2	D	0-0	0-0	38	55,227
34	A	19/3	CHARLTON	8	2	W	2-0	1-0	40	41,415
35	A	23/3	CARDIFF	15	1	W	1-0	1-0	42	16,649
36	H	29/3	SUNDERLAND	6	1	W	2-1	2-0	44	33,203
37	A	2/4	TOTTENHAM	16	1	W	4-2	1-1	46	53,159
38	H	8/4	SHEFFIELD UTD	14	1	D	1-1	0-1	47	50,978
39	H	9/4	WOLVERHAMPTON	3	1	W	1-0	0-0	49	75,043
40	A	16/4	PORTSMOUTH	4	1	D	0-0	0-0	50	40,230
41	H	23/4	SHEFFIELD WED	22	1	W	3-0	1-0	52	51,421
42	A	30/4	MANCHESTER U	5	1	L	1-2	0-1	52	34,933

Average Home 48,308 — Away 32,784

32 — WEST BROM
Saunders 64, Sillett 80, 82p, [Bentley 90] / *Allen 25, 26* — Ref: H Webb
A re-arranged midweek game in the snow is poorly attended. Ronnie Allen's smart poaching is cancelled out by a dramatic late Chelsea rally. Saunders beats the veteran keeper Jim Sanders with a 20-yarder. Sillett nets a deflected free-kick and penalty to sink Vic Buckingham's outfit.
Chelsea: Thomson, Harris, Sillett, Armstrong, Wicks, Saunders, Parsons, McNichol, Bentley, Stubbs, Blunstone
West Brom: *Sanders, Rickaby, Millard, Dudley, Dugdale, Barlow, Griffin, Carter, Allen, Hodgkisson, Lee*

33 — BLACKPOOL
Ref: J Gardner
A disappointing display and the cynics who scoffed at talk of a title challenge have a field day. This was the old Chelsea again, says one paper. Stanley Matthews, now 40, gives Sillett plenty of problems. Stubbs sees one effort cleared off the line. Fans stream away long before the end.
Chelsea: Thomson, Harris, Sillett, Armstrong, Wicks, Saunders, Parsons, McNichol, Bentley, Stubbs, Blunstone
Blackpool: *Farm, Gratrix, Garrett, Fenton, Johnston, Kelly, Matthews, Taylor, Brown, Mudie, Perry*

34 — CHARLTON
Blunstone 12, O'Connell 80 — Ref: K Collinge
O'Connell returns to the team and plays a vital role. Blunstone combines with him before slipping a shot into the corner. Nearly an hour passes before Jimmy Seed's men have a shot. O'Connell clinches the points by chesting down Armstrong's long ball and lashing in a powerful drive.
Chelsea: Thomson, Harris, Sillett, Armstrong, Wicks, Saunders, Parsons, McNichol, Bentley, O'Connell, Blunstone
Charlton: *Bartram, Campbell, Townsend, Hewie, Ufton, Pembery, Hurst, Leary, Ayre, White, Kiernan*

35 — CARDIFF
O'Connell 43 — Ref: B Clements
Trevor Morris' side are sunk by that man O'Connell, who grabs his seventh goal in seven league games as an amateur. Chelsea hang on grimly and go top of the league for the first time since a brief spell early in 1937-38. They're a point clear of Wolves, who have two matches in hand.
Chelsea: Thomson, Harris, Sillett, Armstrong, Wicks, Saunders, Parsons, McNichol, Bentley, O'Connell, Blunstone
Cardiff: *Howells, Rutter, Stitfall, Harrington, Frowen, Sullivan, Nutt, Williams, Ford, Stockin, Northcott*

36 — SUNDERLAND
McDonald 11(og), Willemse 14, Fleming 53 / — Ref: J Williams
Brabrook debuts at 17 and Willemse returns. Blunstone is on England duty and O'Connell injured. A cross is hooked into his own net by Joe McDonald. Moments later Brabrook fires home a Parsons corner. Charlie Fleming's nets a fierce shot, but the visitors' title hopes are in tatters.
Chelsea: Thomson, Harris, Sillett, Armstrong, Wicks, Saunders, Parsons, McNichol, Bentley, Brabrook, Willemse
Sunderland: *Fraser, Hedley, McDonald, Anderson, Daniel, Aitken, Kirtley, Shackleton, Fleming, Chisholm, Elliott*

37 — TOTTENHAM
McNichol 29, 62, Wicks 56, Sillett 68p / *Duquemin 23, 54* — Ref: J Pollard
Len Duquemin nets a fine volley and later a header, but both times rugged Chelsea hit back quickly - via McNichol's half-hit shot and Wicks' close-range header. Sillett's penalty, after a Peter Baker handball, seals the win. Persistent offending by Bentley angers Spurs and he is booked.
Chelsea: Thomson, Harris, Sillett, Dicks, Wicks, Saunders, Parsons, McNichol, Bentley, Brabrook, Willemse
Tottenham: *Reynolds, Baker, Hopkins, Blanchflower, Clarke, Marchi, Gavin, Baily, Duquemin, Brooks, Robb*

38 — SHEFFIELD UTD
Parsons 75 / *Cross 22* — Ref: H Broadhurst
Chelsea go into Easter with a four-point lead but seem to have their minds on tomorrow's big game with Wolves. This display is poor and they look far from title material. Reg Freeman's men take the lead via Jack Cross, but quicksilver Parsons pops up near the end to save a vital point.
Chelsea: Thomson, Harris, Sillett, Armstrong, Wicks, Saunders, Parsons, McNichol, Bentley, Brabrook, Blunstone
Sheffield Utd: *Burgin, Coldwell, Shaw G, Hoyland, Shaw J, Iley, Hawksworth, Hagan, Cross, Rawson, Grainger*

39 — WOLVERHAMPTON
Sillett 74p — Ref: J Malcolm
A lock-out crowd for this potential title 'decider'. The reigning champs are saved by Bert Williams and Bentley misses a sitter. Late in the day, O'Connell's shot is fisted clear by Billy Wright. After consultations, a penalty is given. Sillett blasts it in knee-high to bring the house down.
Chelsea: Thomson, Williams, Sillett, Armstrong, Wicks, Saunders, Parsons, McNichol, Bentley, O'Connell, Blunstone
Wolverhampton: *Williams, Showell, Shorthouse, Slater, Wright, Flowers, Hancocks, Broadbent, Swinbourne, Wilshaw, Smith*

40 — PORTSMOUTH
Ref: R Smith
Eddie Lever's men have games in hand and can still win the title, but a draw would leave Chelsea in a great position. O'Connell is at Wembley with Bishop Auckland, so Stubbs comes in. He sees a drive kicked off the line and has a goal disallowed. All Pompey's pressure is soaked up.
Chelsea: Thomson, Sillett, Harris, Armstrong, Wicks, Saunders, Parsons, McNichol, Bentley, Stubbs, Blunstone
Portsmouth: *Uprichard, McGhee, Mansell, Pickett, Reid, Dickinson, Harris, Gordon, Henderson, Rafferty, Newman*

41 — SHEFFIELD WED
Parsons 22, 77, Sillett 72p — Ref: B Ling
A win over relegated Wednesday, plus Pompey not winning at Cardiff, will clinch the title today. Parsons settles nerves with a header. David McIntosh is carried off with a back injury and stand-in Norman Curtis is beaten twice. Pompey only draw, so the celebrations can commence!
Chelsea: Thomson, Sillett, Harris, Armstrong, Wicks, Saunders, Parsons, McNichol, Bentley, O'Connell, Blunstone
Sheffield Wed: *McIntosh, Martin, Curtis, McAnearney, McEvoy, Kay, Finney, Quixall, Froggatt, Sewell, Marriott*

42 — MANCHESTER U
Bentley 82 / *Taylor 84, Scanlon 32* — Ref: R Mann
United sportingly applaud the new champions onto the field but Matt Busby's men are in no mood to relax. Tommy Taylor scores a deserved opening goal. Bentley's header from a Blunstone centre equalises, but Albert Scanlon takes Taylor's pass and sprints clear to net a late winner.
Chelsea: Thomson, Sillett, Harris, Armstrong, Wicks, Saunders, Parsons, McNichol, Bentley, O'Connell, Blunstone
Manchester U: *Wood, Foulkes, Byrne, Gibson, Jones, Goodwin, Berry, Blanchflower, Taylor, Viollet, Scanlon*

LEAGUE DIVISION 1 (CUP-TIES) Manager: Ted Drake

FA Cup

	Att Pos	F-A	H-T	Scorers, Times, and Referees	1	2	3	4	5	6	7	8	9	10	11
3 H WALSALL 8/1	4 W 40,020 3S:20	2-0	1-0	O'Connell 17, Stubbs 60 Ref: G Pullin	Robertson *Baldwin*	Sillett *Guttridge*	Willemse *Vinall*	Armstrong *Crook*	Wicks *McPherson*	Saunders *Tarrant*	Parsons *Morris*	O'Connell *Dorman*	Bentley *Richards*	Stubbs *Myerscough*	Blunstone *Meek*

Major Frank Butler's team are bottom of the Third Division (South), but they overcome the setback of an early goal to get stronger. Veteran ex-West Brom keeper Harry Baldwin, rescued from non-league Kettering, plays a starring role and this is certainly no walkover for Chelsea.

	Att Pos	F-A	H-T	Scorers, Times, and Referees	1	2	3	4	5	6	7	8	9	10	11
4 A BRISTOL ROV 29/1	6 W 35,952 2:12	3-1	3-0	Parsons 4, McNichol 23, Blunstone 42 *Pitt 60p* Ref: M Griffiths	Thomson *Radford*	Sillett *Bamford*	Willemse *Fox*	Armstrong *Pitt*	Wicks *Warren*	Saunders *Cairney*	Parsons *Petheridge*	McNichol *Roost*	Bentley *Lambden*	Stubbs *Bradford*	Lewis *Watling*

A record Eastville crowd sees Howard Radford parry Blunstone's cross to Parsons, who nets the first. Blunstone and Bentley set up McNichol for another and Blunstone settles the outcome, burying a fierce drive. Jack Pitt scores from the spot after John Watling is clattered by Sillett.

	Att Pos	F-A	H-T	Scorers, Times, and Referees	1	2	3	4	5	6	7	8	9	10	11
5 A NOTTS CO 19/2	6 L 41,930 2:6	0-1	0-0	*Broadbent 51* Ref: J Clough	Thomson *Bradley*	Sillett *Southwell*	Willemse *Deans*	Armstrong *Adamson*	Wicks *Leuty*	Saunders *Johnston*	Parsons *Wills*	McNichol *Wylie*	Bentley *Jackson*	Stubbs *Leverton*	Lewis *Broadbent*

On a treacherous icy pitch, Ron Wylie picks up a clearance, avoids two challenges and sends a pass to Jim Jackson, who misses the ball, but Albert Broadbent steps in to crash a shot past Thomson. Parsons misses an open goal and George Poyser's men hang on to reach the last eight.

Tour match

	Att Pos	F-A	H-T	Scorers, Times, and Referees	1	2	3	4	5	6	7	8	9	10	11
H RED BANNER (Hungary) 15/12	4 D 41,452	2-2	2-1	Bentley 42, Stubbs 43 *Hidegkuti 18, Palotas 60* Ref: A Bond	Robertson *Olah*	Harris *Kovacs J*	Willemse *Borzsey*	Armstrong *Lantos*	Greenwood *Kovacs I*	Saunders *Zakarias*	Parsons *Sandor*	McNichol *Hidegkuti*	Bentley *Palotas*	Stubbs *Szolnok*	Blunstone *Toth*

TV cameras and a big midweek afternoon crowd greet a crack side full of internationals. Nandor Hidegkuti and Peter Palotas' goals are superb, but the game is not a great spectacle. Three penalties are missed in 12 minutes: Harris (one wide, one saved) and Lantos (wide) are the culprits.

		P	W	D	L	Home F	A	W	D	L	Away F	A	Pts
1	CHELSEA	42	11	5	5	43	29	9	7	5	38	28	52
2	Wolves	42	13	5	3	58	30	6	5	10	31	40	48
3	Portsmouth	42	13	5	3	44	21	5	7	9	30	41	48
4	Sunderland	42	8	11	2	39	27	7	7	7	25	27	48
5	Manchester U	42	12	4	5	44	30	8	3	10	40	44	47
6	Aston Villa	42	11	3	7	38	31	9	4	8	34	42	47
7	Manchester C	42	11	5	5	45	36	7	5	9	31	33	46
8	Newcastle	42	12	5	4	53	27	5	4	12	36	50	43
9	Arsenal	42	12	3	6	44	25	5	6	10	22	38	43
10	Burnley	42	11	3	7	29	19	6	6	9	25	29	43
11	Everton	42	9	6	6	32	24	4	7	10	30	44	42
12	Huddersfield	42	10	4	7	28	23	4	9	8	35	45	41
13	Sheffield Utd	42	10	3	8	41	34	7	4	10	29	52	41
14	Preston	42	8	5	8	47	33	8	3	10	36	31	40
15	Charlton	42	8	6	7	43	34	7	4	10	33	41	40
16	Tottenham	42	9	4	8	42	35	7	4	10	30	38	40
17	West Brom	42	11	5	5	44	33	5	3	13	32	63	40
18	Bolton	42	11	6	4	45	29	2	7	12	17	40	39
19	Blackpool	42	8	6	7	33	26	6	4	11	27	38	38
20	Cardiff	42	9	4	8	41	38	4	7	10	21	38	37
21	Leicester	42	9	6	6	43	32	3	5	13	31	54	35
22	Sheffield Wed	42	7	7	7	42	38	1	3	17	21	62	26
		924	223	111	128	918	654	128	111	223	654	918	924

Odds & ends

Double wins: (5) Bolton, Newcastle, Sheff Utd, Tottenham, Wolves.

Double losses: (1) Manchester U.

Won from behind: (4) Bolton (h), Huddersfield (h), WBA (a). Spurs (a).

Lost from in front: (1) Manchester U (h).

High spots: Winning a first major trophy in the club's 'Golden Jubilee'.

The eleven-goal thriller with Manchester United.

Doing the 'double' over reigning champions Wolves.

The side keeping its nerve – and clean sheets – in the tense April games against Wolves and Pompey.

The highest average home crowds in the country.

Low spots: Five successive penalties missed mid-season.

The criticism from many quarters for 'rugged' tactics.

Chelsea's title-winning tally of 52 points remains the lowest since 42-match seasons commenced in 1919.

Hat-tricks: (2) O'Connell (v Man U); Roy Bentley (v Newcastle).

Opposing hat-tricks: (1) Dennis Violett (Man U).

Ever-presents: (2) Eric Parsons, Derek Saunders.

Leading scorer: (21) Roy Bentley.

Appearances / Goals

	Lge	FAC	Lge	FAC	Tot
	Appearances		**Goals**		
Armstrong, Ken	39	3	1		1
Bentley, Roy	41	3	21		21
Blunstone, Frank	23	3	3	1	4
Brabrook, Peter	3				
Dicks, Alan	1				
Edwards, Robert	1				
Greenwood, Ron	21				
Harris, John	31				
Lewis, Jim	17		6		6
McNichol, Johnny	40	2	14	1	15
O'Connell, Seamus	10	1	7	1	8
Parsons, Eric	42	3	11	1	12
Robertson, Bill	26	1			
Saunders, Derek	42	3	1		1
Sillett, Peter	21	3	6		6
Smith, Bobby	4				
Stubbs, Les	27	3	5	1	6
Thomson, Charlie	16	2			
Wicks, Stan	21	3	1		1
Willemse, Stan	36	3	1		1
(own-goals)			4		4
20 players used	462	33	81	5	86

LEAGUE DIVISION 1   Manager: Ted Drake   SEASON 1955-56

No	Date	Att	Pos	Pt	F-A	H-T	Scorers, Times, and Referees	1	2	3	4	5	6	7	8	9	10	11
1	H BOLTON 20/8	44,454	L	0	0-2	0:1	Stevens 22, Holden 65 Ref: B Buckle	Thomson	Sillett	Willemse	Armstrong	Wicks	Saunders	Parsons	McNichol	Bentley	O'Connell	Blunstone
								Grieves	*Ball*	*Banks*	*Wheeler*	*Barrass*	*Edwards*	*Holden*	*Moir*	*Lofthouse*	*Stevens*	*Parry*

The championship trophy is paraded around the ground before kick-off, but Bill Ridding's boys spoil the party. Dennis Stevens finds space to net from 25 yards. Ray Parry's cross is driven in first time by Doug Holden. Bentley hits a post, but the champs generally look in poor shape.

No	Date	Att	Pos	Pt	F-A	H-T	Scorers, Times, and Referees	1	2	3	4	5	6	7	8	9	10	11
2	A HUDDERSFIELD 24/8	28,308	15	W 2	3-1	2-0	Blunstone 29, O'Con'l 31, Parsons 49 Glazzard 61 Ref: F Overton	Thomson	Sillett	Willemse	Armstrong	Wicks	Saunders	Parsons	McNichol	Bentley	O'Connell	Blunstone
								Mills	*McGarry*	*Kelly*	*Battye*	*Cockerill*	*Quested*	*Marriott*	*Watson*	*Glazzard*	*Frear*	*Simpson*

Debutant Ron Cockerill's miskick leads to Blunstone firing the first. Then Blunstone's shot flies in off O'Connell. Parsons wraps it up after a Blunstone shot is parried. Looking offside, Jimmy Glazzard crashes in Bryan Frear's pass. Terriers' boss Andy Beattie quits after the match.

No	Date	Att	Pos	Pt	F-A	H-T	Scorers, Times, and Referees	1	2	3	4	5	6	7	8	9	10	11
3	H ARSENAL 27/8	36,034	10	D 3	1-1	1-0	O'Connell 5 Lawton 67 Ref: B Clements	Thomson	Sillett	Willemse	Armstrong	Wicks	Saunders	Parsons	McNichol	Bentley	O'Connell	Blunstone
								Kelsey	*Barnes*	*Evans*	*Goring*	*Fotheringham*	*Bowen*	*Clapton*	*Tapscott*	*Lawton*	*Lishman*	*Roper*

Sillett's lob is headed home by O'Connell. Chelsea look inventive early on, but the game slowly deteriorates. Saunders trips Derek Tapscott, but Dennis Evans' penalty is saved by Thomson. The keeper then fumbles Danny Clapton's drive and Tommy Lawton bags a soft equaliser.

No	Date	Att	Pos	Pt	F-A	H-T	Scorers, Times, and Referees	1	2	3	4	5	6	7	8	9	10	11
4	H HUDDERSFIELD 29/8	25,983	10	D 4	0-0	0-0	Ref: F Overton	Thomson	Sillett	Willemse	Armstrong	Wicks	Saunders	Parsons	McNichol	Bentley	O'Connell	Blunstone
								Mills	*Gibson*	*Conwell*	*McGarry*	*Taylor*	*Quested*	*Marriott*	*Watson*	*Glazzard*	*Cavanagh*	*Metcalfe*

Stamford Bridge breaks into slow-handclapping during this lack-lustre display. Huddersfield's wayward shooting saves Chelsea from a shock loss. The champions lack imagination and are often caught offside. Parsons misses a late chance, being robbed as he tries to walk the ball in.

No	Date	Att	Pos	Pt	F-A	H-T	Scorers, Times, and Referees	1	2	3	4	5	6	7	8	9	10	11
5	H PORTSMOUTH 3/9	44,273	16	L 4	1-5	0-3	O'Connell 83 *(Rees 40, 52)* Harris 20, 85, Henderson 36, Ref: R Mann	Thomson	Sillett	Willemse	Nicholas	Wicks	Saunders	Parsons	McNichol	Bentley	O'Connell	Blunstone
								Uprichard	*McGhee*	*Mansell*	*Gunter*	*Reid*	*Dickinson*	*Harris*	*Pickett*	*Henderson*	*Rees*	*Neil*

Eddie Lever's men make monkeys of the champions. Peter Harris lobs over stranded Thomson and Jackie Henderson thunders in a 30-yarder. It gets worse as Derek Rees capitalises on defensive chaos for the third, then drives in another. Harris dribbles round Thomson near the end.

No	Date	Att	Pos	Pt	F-A	H-T	Scorers, Times, and Referees	1	2	3	4	5	6	7	8	9	10	11
6	A BLACKPOOL 5/9	30,563	20	L 4	1-2	1-1	Brabrook 44 Fenton 8p, Mortensen 58 Ref: E Oxley	Robertson	Sillett	Willemse	Armstrong	Wicks	Saunders	Lewis	Brabrook	Bentley	Stubbs	Blunstone
								Farm	*Shimwell*	*Wright*	*Fenton*	*Gratrix*	*Kelly H*	*Matthews*	*Taylor*	*Mortensen*	*Mudie*	*Perry*

Drake rings the changes after the Pompey debacle. Willemse does a good job marking Stan Matthews. Wicks' foul allows Ewan Fenton to net a penalty. Brabrook notches a fine equaliser. Matthews' quick throw releases Eddie Shimwell to cross for Mortensen to head the winning goal.

No	Date	Att	Pos	Pt	F-A	H-T	Scorers, Times, and Referees	1	2	3	4	5	6	7	8	9	10	11
7	A SUNDERLAND 10/9	45,241	19	L 4	3-4	3-1	Bentley 2, Stubbs 21, 26 Fleming 44,48, Chisholm 56, 85 Ref: J Topliss	Robertson	Sillett	Willemse	Nicholas	Wicks	Saunders	Parsons	Brabrook	Bentley	Stubbs	Blunstone
								Fraser	*Stelling*	*Hudgell*	*Anderson*	*Daniel*	*Aitken*	*Bingham*	*Fleming*	*Purdon*	*Chisholm*	*Shackleton*

Bentley fires home in the early stages and Stubbs punishes a Bill Fraser blunder. Chelsea go three up as Stubbs powers in his second. Charlie Fleming pulls one back to signal an amazing collapse. Len Shackleton is magnificent and sets up the late winner, headed in by Ken Chisholm.

No	Date	Att	Pos	Pt	F-A	H-T	Scorers, Times, and Referees	1	2	3	4	5	6	7	8	9	10	11
8	H ASTON VILLA 17/9	35,221	19	D 5	0-0	0-0	Ref: J McLoughlin	Robertson	Sillett	Willemse	Armstrong	Wicks	Saunders	Parsons	Brabrook	Bentley	Stubbs	Blunstone
								Jones	*Lynn*	*Aldis*	*Baxter*	*Martin*	*Moss*	*Southren*	*Dixon*	*Hickson*	*Crowe*	*McParland*

Villa are predictable and Chelsea look anxious. The result is an aimless, ragged affair. Con Martin blocks a Blunstone effort on the line and Vic Crowe hits a post at the other end. Robertson makes a fine save to prevent a Sillett own goal. Young winger Brabrook looks a promising talent.

No	Date	Att	Pos	Pt	F-A	H-T	Scorers, Times, and Referees	1	2	3	4	5	6	7	8	9	10	11
9	A WOLVERHAMPTON 24/9	43,017	21	L 5	1-2	1-1	Parsons 8 Swinbourne 37, 69 Ref: H Webb	Robertson	Sillett	Willemse	Armstrong	Wicks	Saunders	Parsons	McNichol	Bentley	Smith	Blunstone
								Williams	*Stuart*	*Shorthouse*	*Slater*	*Flowers*	*Clamp*	*Hancocks*	*Booth*	*Swinbourne*	*Wilshaw*	*Mullen*

Chelsea start well but Smith treads on the ball when Bentley sets up an open-goal chance. Bentley slices a chance off target before setting up Parsons to net an angled drive. Eddie Clamp's long ball is converted by Roy Swinbourne. Bill Shorthouse's solo run sets up a deserved winner.

No	Date	Att	Pos	Pt	F-A	H-T	Scorers, Times, and Referees	1	2	3	4	5	6	7	8	9	10	11
10	H MANCHESTER C 1/10	44,582	19	W 7	2-1	1-1	McNichol 40, Smith 83 Marsden 29 Ref: M Griffiths	Robertson	Sillett	Willemse	Armstrong	Wicks	Saunders	Parsons	McNichol	Bentley	Smith	Blunstone
								Trautmann	*Branagan*	*Little*	*Barnes*	*Ewing*	*Phoenix*	*Spurdle*	*Hayes*	*Johnstone*	*Marsden*	*Fagan*

Les McDowall's men miss the influence of absent Don Revie. Bert Trautmann is kept very busy. City new boy Ken Marsden taps home the opening goal after a mix-up. Bentley sets up McNichol's leveller and Bentley's lob is headed in by the unmarked Smith. Huge relief all round.

Match summaries

#	V	Opponent	Date	Att	Pos	Opp Pos	Res	Score	HT	Pts	Scorers	Ref
11	A	CHARLTON	8/10	40,980	16	5	W	2-1	0-0	9	Smith 57, 83; *Gauld 90*	H Haworth
12	H	TOTTENHAM	15/10	48,195	14	22	W	2-0	1-0	11	Smith 35, Bentley 82	L Callaghan
13	A	PRESTON	22/10	**17,799**	12	13	W	3-2	0-1	13	Pars'ns 52, Bentley 77, Doch'ty 63 (og); *Thompson 26, 70*	G Oliver
14	H	BURNLEY	29/10	39,069	13	8	D	0-0	0-0	14		R Wood
15	A	BIRMINGHAM	5/11	30,499	14	8	L	0-3	0-2	14	*Astall 2, 43, Boyd 47*	K Dagnall
16	H	WEST BROM	12/11	41,888	14	6	W	2-0	0-0	16	Tindall 62, Sillett 63	W Gaiger
17	A	MANCHESTER U	19/11	22,192	15	2	L	0-3	0-0	16	*Byrne 46p, Taylor 52, 68*	J Gardner
18	H	SHEFFIELD UTD	26/11	30,032	14	20	W	1-0	1-0	18	Bentley 21	J Swain
19	A	EVERTON	3/12	33,473	14	10	D	3-3	2-0	19	Parsons 30, 88, Brabrook 31; *Harris 46, Jones 70, Eglington 75*	S Rogers
20	H	NEWCASTLE	10/12	37,327	12	14	W	2-1	1-1	21	Brabrook 24, Tindall 88; *Milburn 35p*	N Hough
21	A	BOLTON	17/12	24,129	13	5	L	0-4	0-2	21	*Lofthouse 35, 50, 80, Gubbins 42*	B Buckle

Line-ups (Chelsea / *Opponent*)

11 Charlton (A): Robertson, Sillett, Willemse, Armstrong, Wicks, Saunders, Parsons, McNichol, Bentley, Smith, Blunstone / *Bartram, Campbell, Townsend, Hewie, Utton, Hammond, Hurst, Gauld, Leary, White, Kiernan*

12 Tottenham (H): Robertson, Sillett, Willemse, Armstrong, Wicks, Saunders, Parsons, McNichol, Bentley, Smith, Blunstone / *Ditchburn, Baker, Hopkins, Blanchflower, Clarke, Marchi, Walters, Brooks, Duquemin, McClellan, Dyson*

13 Preston (A): Robertson, Sillett, Willemse, Armstrong, Wicks, Saunders, Parsons, McNichol, Bentley, Smith, Blunstone / *Thompson G, Cunningham, Wilson, Docherty, Mattinson, Dunn, Campbell, Thompson T, Hatsell, Baxter, Morrison*

14 Burnley (H): Robertson, Sillett, Willemse, Armstrong, Wicks, Saunders, Parsons, McNichol, Bentley, Smith, Blunstone / *McDonald, Rudman, Winton, Seith, Cummings, Shannon, Gray, McIlroy, McKay, Cheesebrough, Pilkington*

15 Birmingham (A): Robertson, Sillett, Willemse, Armstrong, Wicks, Saunders, Parsons, McNichol, Bentley, Smith, Blunstone / *Merrick, Hall, Badham, Boyd, Smith, Warhurst, Astall, Kinsey, Brown, Murphy, Govan*

16 West Brom (H): Robertson, Sillett, Willemse, Armstrong, Wicks, Saunders, Parsons, Brabrook, Bentley, **Tindall**, Blunstone / *Sanders, Williams, Millard, Dudley, Kennedy, Brooks, Griffin, Carter, Allen, Nicholls, Lee*

17 Manchester U (A): Robertson, Sillett, Willemse, Armstrong, Wicks, Saunders, Parsons, Brabrook, Bentley, Tindall, Blunstone / *Wood, Foulkes, Byrne, Colman, Jones, Edwards, Berry, Doherty, Taylor, Viollet, Pegg*

18 Sheffield Utd (H): Robertson, Sillett, Willemse, Armstrong, Wicks, Saunders, Parsons, Brabrook, Bentley, Tindall, Blunstone / *Hodgkinson, Coldwell, Mason, Shaw, Johnson, Iley, Ringstead, Waldock, Wragg, Hewitt, Grainger*

19 Everton (A): Robertson, Sillett, Willemse, Armstrong, Wicks, Saunders, Parsons, Brabrook, Bentley, Tindall, Blunstone / *O'Neill, Moore, Tansey, Farrell, Jones, Lello, McNamara, Wainwright, Harris, Parker, Eglington*

20 Newcastle (H): Robertson, Sillett, Willemse, Armstrong, Wicks, Saunders, Parsons, Brabrook, Bentley, Tindall, Blunstone / *Simpson, Batty, McMichael, Scoular, Stokoe, Crowe, White, Davies, Keeble, Milburn, Punton*

21 Bolton (A): Robertson, Sillett, Willemse, Armstrong, Wicks, Saunders, Parsons, Brabrook, Bentley, Tindall, Blunstone / *Grieves, Hartle, Banks, Wheeler, Barrass, Edwards, Holden, Stevens, Lofthouse, Parry, Gubbins*

Match reports

11 Charlton: The terrible start to the season is behind them and the fast-improving Smith bags two more goals. His first scrapes inside a post after Bentley's pass, and the second sees him pounce on poor defensive work. Jimmy Seed's high-flying side scramble a late consolation through Jim Gauld.

12 Tottenham: New boss Jimmy Anderson has overseen just two wins from 12 and there is unrest at Spurs due to a wages dispute. They give Chelsea no real bother, although Terry Dyson looks lively. A Saunders shot goes in off Smith's heel. Bentley's superb 18-yard drive is the match's highlight.

13 Preston: The revival continues, aided by both PNE wingers getting injured. When a Sillett penalty is turned against the bar, Parsons buries the rebound. Tommy Docherty turns a Parsons cross into his own net. Tommy Thompson nets a neat goal but Bentley heads in Blunstone's cross to win it.

14 Burnley: Chelsea look rather casual and Parsons is the only man to give Alan Brown's men much trouble. Sillett ventures forward and crashes a typical effort against the bar. Parsons and McNichol also hit wood. The club announces plans to spend £20,000 on installing floodlights at the Bridge.

15 Birmingham: Arthur Turner's Second Division champions are well on top. Gordon Astall cuts in and nets after an early free-kick routine. Just an Astall effort, but he forces the rebound past Robertson. The match is settled when Londoner Len Boyd thunders home a superb 30-yarder.

16 West Brom: The ref mysteriously plays 49 minutes in the first half. Ron Tindall, 20, debuts in place of Smith and pounces to scramble in a debut goal. Just seconds later Sillett sends a 35-yard free-kick past Jim Saunders. Tindall looks a decent prospect and Smith will soon join Spurs for £20,000.

17 Manchester U: Resistance crumbles after the break as Derek Saunders handles and Roger Byrne converts the penalty. Tommy Taylor dribbles past Robertson to net a fine solo goal. Ray Wood takes the ball off Bentley's toe, punts upfield and Wicks misses the winning goal until Parsons pounces to convert a Brabrook pass.

18 Sheffield Utd: In his 300th League game for the Blues, Bentley collects a Sillett lob and lofts a shot over Alan Hodgkinson. Joe Mercer's side get the chance to level via a 52nd-minute controversial penalty, after Alf Ringstead's drive hit Wicks' arm. Peter Wragg's effort is well saved by Robertson.

19 Everton: Parsons nets after a Tommy Jones error and moments later Brabrook steers in Blunstone's cross. Jimmy Harris converts a cross for Everton's first and then helps create an equaliser. Eglington's left-foot shot looks like the winning goal until Parsons pounces to convert a Brabrook pass.

20 Newcastle: Tindall twice has shots blocked but the ball falls to Parsons, who sets up a Brabrook headed goal. Willemse handles on the line to prevent Len White scoring and Jackie Milburn nets the penalty. After Bob Stokoe and Ron Batty fail to clear the ball, Tindall nips in to bury a fierce shot.

21 Bolton: Lofthouse – 'the Lion of Vienna' – is in fine form and dives to head in a Ray Parry cross. Ralph Gubbins nets another after Robertson fumbled. Doug Holden crosses for another Lofthouse headed goal and the England centre-forward completes his hat-trick with a powerful run and shot.

LEAGUE DIVISION 1   Manager: Ted Drake   SEASON 1955-56

No	Date	Att	Pos	Pt	F-A	H-T	Scorers, Times, and Referees	1	2	3	4	5	6	7	8	9	10	11
22	H ARSENAL 24/12	43,022	11 W 17	23	2-0	2-0	Bentley 21, Blunstone 35 — Ref: B Clements	Robertson / *Sullivan*	Sillett / *Charlton*	Willemse / *Evans*	Armstrong / *Goring*	Wicks / *Fotheringham*	Saunders / *Holton*	Parsons / *Clapton*	McNichol / *Tapscott*	Bentley / *Groves*	Stubbs / *Bloomfield*	Blunstone / *Tiddy*
23	A CARDIFF 26/12	26,794	12 D 18	24	1-1	1-1	Bentley 24 / *Sherwood 30p* — Ref: H Broadhurst	Robertson / *Howells*	Sillett / *Davies*	Willemse / *Sherwood*	Armstrong / *Harrington*	Wicks / *Malloy*	Saunders / *Baker*	Parsons / *Walsh*	McNichol / *Kirtley*	Bentley / *Hitchens*	Stubbs / *O'Halloran*	Blunstone / *McSeveney*
24	H CARDIFF 27/12	26,740	11 W 18	26	2-1	0-0	McNichol 52, Stubbs 80 / *Hitchens 88* — Ref: H Broadhurst	Robertson / *Howells*	Sillett / *Stittall*	Willemse / *Sherwood*	Armstrong / *Harrington*	Wicks / *Malloy*	Saunders / *Baker*	Parsons / *Kirtley*	McNichol / *Hitchens*	Bentley / *Ford*	Stubbs / *O'Halloran*	Blunstone / *Nugent*
25	A PORTSMOUTH 31/12	22,995	9 D 6	27	4-4	3-2	Blunstone 5, 11, 49, Stubbs 35 / *Henderson 38, 45, Harris 56, 84* — Ref: R Mann	Robertson / *Uprichard*	Sillett / *McGhee*	Willemse / *Mansell*	Armstrong / *Pickett*	Wicks / *Gunter*	Saunders / *Dickinson*	Parsons / *Harris*	McNichol / *Gordon*	Bentley / *Henderson*	Stubbs / *Barnard*	Blunstone / *Dale*
26	H SUNDERLAND 14/1	43,999	12 L 4	27	2-3	1-2	Bone 40 (og), Bentley 52 / *Fleming 24, Shackleton 31, Elliott 51* — Ref: J Topliss	Robertson / *Fraser*	Sillett / *Hedley*	Willemse / *McDonald*	Armstrong / *Anderson*	Wicks / *Bone*	Saunders / *Aitken*	Parsons / *Kemp*	McNichol / *Fleming*	Bentley / *Holden*	Stubbs / *Elliott*	Blunstone / *Shackleton*
27	A ASTON VILLA 21/1	24,232	11 W 21	29	4-1	1-1	Stubbs 20, 75, Blunstone 47, *Lynn 15p* [Parsons 62] — Ref: J McLoughlin	Robertson / *Jones*	Sillett / *Lynn*	Willemse / *Aldis*	Dicks / *Hogg*	Wicks / *Ashfield*	Saunders / *Crowe*	Parsons / *Roberts*	McNichol / *Sewell*	Tindall / *Dixon*	Stubbs / *McParland*	Blunstone / *Lockhart*
28	H WOLVERHAMPTON 4/2	37,170	13 L 4	29	2-3	1-1	Tindall 10, 80 / *Broadbent 15, 85, Murray 74* — Ref: H Webb	Robertson / *Williams*	Sillett / *Stuart*	Willemse / *Shorthouse*	Dicks / *Slater*	Wicks / *Wright*	Saunders / *Clamp*	Parsons / *Hancocks*	Brabrook / *Broadbent*	Tindall / *Murray*	Stubbs / *Wilshaw*	Blunstone / *Deeley*
29	A MANCHESTER C 11/2	26,642	13 D 8	30	2-2	0-2	Lewis 69, O'Connell 89 / *Hayes 19, 31* — Ref: M Griffiths	Robertson / *Trautmann*	**Bellett** / *Leivers*	Willemse / *Little*	**Nicholas** / *Barnes*	Wicks / *Ewing*	Saunders / *Paul*	Lewis / *Spurdle*	Brabrook / *Hayes*	Tindall / *Johnstone*	O'Connell / *Dyson*	**Kitchener** / *Clarke*
30	H CHARLTON 22/2	8,473	8 W 14	32	3-1	2-0	Tindall 15, 43, Bentley 76 / *Ayre 75* — Ref: H Haworth	Thomson / *Bartram*	Harris / *Campbell*	Willemse / *Ellis*	Nicholas / *O'Lynn*	Wicks / *Hewie*	Saunders / *Ufton*	Lewis / *Ayre*	McNichol / *Gauld*	Bentley / *Leary*	Tindall / *Ryan*	Blunstone / *Kiernan*
31	A TOTTENHAM 25/2	46,767	11 L 19	32	0-4	0-1	*Brooks 15, 81 Smith 54, Marchi 60* — Ref: L Callaghan	Thomson / *Reynolds*	Sillett / *Norman*	Willemse / *Hopkins*	Nicholas / *Blanchflower*	Wicks / *Clarke*	Saunders / *Marchi*	Lewis / *Harmer*	McNichol / *Brooks*	Bentley / *Duquemin*	Tindall / *Smith*	Blunstone / *Robb*

22 — H ARSENAL: Chelsea move back into the top half of the table at last, and are on top against Tom Whittaker's men. Parsons skips across the mud to cross for Bentley to head in. Bentley's centre is then netted by Blunstone. Bobby Smith has left for Spurs and scores on his debut today against Luton.

23 — A CARDIFF: Bentley escapes his marker to crack home the opening goal and stun Ninian Park. Minutes later Willemse deliberately handles a goal-bound shot to concede a penalty equaliser. Trevor Morris's Bluebirds have the majority of the play overall, but look hesitant and shot-shy in attack.

24 — H CARDIFF: McNichol tucks the ball in from close range to put Chelsea ahead. Stubbs pounces on poor defending to make the points safe. Promising young centre-forward Gerry Hitchens grabs a consolation goal that the lack-lustre visitors hardly deserve. Man of the match is wing-half Armstrong.

25 — A PORTSMOUTH: Chelsea waste a 3-0 lead. Blunstone stabs in and then converts after Bentley's run. Stubbs nets from Blunstone's pass, but Jackie Henderson bags two well-taken goals before the break. Blunstone completes his hat-trick, but Peter Harris strikes twice in a thrilling rally to save the day.

26 — H SUNDERLAND: Len Shackleton sets up a Charlie Fleming goal before scoring himself with a touch of genius. From near the corner flag, he sidesteps three men before dummying the keeper. Jim Bone heads Sillett's lob into his own net. Billy Elliott makes it three, then Bentley surges in to pull one back.

27 — A ASTON VILLA: Dicks is called up after Armstrong goes down with pleurisy. Jackie Sewell is blocked by Willemse for Villa's opener from the spot. Stubbs levels and after the break defensive lapses allow Chelsea's first win here since the War. It appears only a miracle will save Villa from the drop.

28 — H WOLVERHAMPTON: In atrocious wintry conditions, this is one of the few games to go ahead today. Bentley is rested and Willemse made skipper. Tindall buries a Brabrook pass, but Peter Broadbent levels and hits a late winner after Tindall made it 2-2 late on. Hero of this thriller is keeper Bert Williams.

29 — A MANCHESTER C: Drake rings the changes: Veteran Harris is recalled; Walter Bellett (ex-Barking) and Ray Kitchener (ex-Hitchin) get debuts. Les McDowall's men surge ahead via two drives from Joe Hayes. Lewis pulls one back from close in. O'Connell darts in to snatch a dramatic late point-saver.

30 — H CHARLTON: A re-arranged game on a cold Wednesday afternoon draws a poor crowd. Tindall defies the icy pitch and swivels to fire a fine opener. Bentley and Lewis set up his second. Bob Ayre nets after Buck Ryan's shot is blocked. Bentley heads in to finish off Jimmy Seed's outfit.

31 — A TOTTENHAM: Spurs are dominant and Johnny Brooks fires in lively Tommy Harmer's chipped pass. Bobby Smith, sold by Chelsea recently, cracks home a tremendous volley. A 35-yard lob by Tony Marchi drifts in, with Thomson seemingly impeded. The keeper makes a bad error for the fourth.

Chelsea match-by-match record (1956–57), matches 32–42

No	V	Date	Opponent	Pos	Res	Score	Att	Opp Pos	Pts
32	H	3/3	MANCHESTER U	13	L	2-4	32,050	1	32
33	A	10/3	BURNLEY	16	L	0-5	18,670	9	32
34	H	21/3	BIRMINGHAM	17	L	1-2	12,637	5	32
35	A	24/3	WEST BROM	17	L	0-2	20,219	10	32
36	A	30/3	LUTON	18	D	2-2	24,276	6	33
37	H	31/3	PRESTON	18	L	0-1	31,450	15	33
38	H	2/4	LUTON	18	D	0-0	26,364	12	34
39	A	7/4	SHEFFIELD UTD	18	L	1-2	23,398	19	34
40	H	14/4	EVERTON	18	W	6-1	13,825	15	36
41	A	21/4	NEWCASTLE	17	D	1-1	24,322	11	37
42	H	28/4	BLACKPOOL	16	W	2-1	35,427	2	39

Home 36,800 · Away 27,655 · Average 32,...

---

32. H Manchester U — 2-4
Scorers: Parsons 21, Bentley 24 / Pegg 34, Viollet 56, 67, Taylor 89
Ref: J Gardner
Chelsea: Robertson, Sillett, Willemse, Nicholas, Wicks, Saunders, Parsons, Brabrook, Bentley, Tindall, Blunstone
Manchester U: Wood, Greaves, Byrne, Colman, Jones, Edwards, Berry, Whelan, Taylor, Viollet, Pegg
Chelsea lead at the interval, with great work by Bentley setting up a Parsons header and Bentley then volleying in a corner. John Berry sets up Dennis Viollet's leveller, the latter flicking United ahead from Dave Pegg's cross. The leaders finish the job when Tommy Taylor wallops in.

33. A Burnley — 0-5
Scorers: Pilkington 49, 62, 72 / Cheesebrough 35, McKay 67
Ref: R Wood
Chelsea: Robertson, Sillett, Bellett, Nicholas, Wicks, Saunders, Parsons, Brabrook, Bentley, Tindall, Blunstone
Burnley: McDonald, Cummings, Winton, Seith, Adamson, Shannon, Newlands, McIlroy, McKay, Cheesebrough, Pilkington
Allan Brown's men gain easy revenge for their defeat in the recent five-game cup marathon. Sillett has a nightmare against tricky winger Brian Pilkington, who grabs a hat-trick. One of his trio is a lucky deflection off Nicholas. A rare Wicks error lets in Peter McKay for the fourth goal.

34. H Birmingham — 1-2
Scorers: Stubbs 29 / Govan 42, Kinsey 84
Ref: K Dagnall
Chelsea: Robertson, Sillett, Willemse, Nicholas, Wicks, Saunders, Parsons, McNichol, Bentley, Stubbs, Blunstone
Birmingham: Merrick, Hall, Badham, Boyd, Smith, Warhurst, Astall, Kinsey, Brown, Murphy, Govan
Another low crowd due to the midweek afternoon kick-off. Stubbs nets with Gil Merrick pleading he was impeded. Extrovert Eddie Brown puts on a fine show for Arthur Turner's cup finalists and sets up Alex Govan's equaliser. Brown's free-kick finds Noel Kinsey for the winner.

35. A West Brom — 0-2
Scorers: — / Nicholls 27, 70, Griffin 31
Ref: W Gaiger
Chelsea: Robertson, Sillett, Willemse, Saunders, Wicks, Casey, Parsons, McNichol, Bentley, Stubbs, Blunstone
West Brom: Sanders, Howe, Millard, Dudley, Barlow, Summers, Griffin, Robson, Allen, Nicholls, Lee
Len Casey debuts, nearly three years after signing. New in Vic Buckingham's side is Bobby Robson, signed from Fulham. Chelsea's slump goes on as John Nicholls nets at the second attempt, then Robson sets up Frank Griffin. Nicholls grabs the third after Ronnie Allen hits a post.

36. A Luton — 2-2
Scorers: Sillett 52p, Dicks 57 / Gregory 36, Davies 46
Ref: F Coultas
Chelsea: Robertson, Sillett, Willemse, Dicks, Wicks, Casey, Parsons, McNichol, Bentley, Stubbs, Blunstone
Luton: Baynham, Dunne, Jones, Morton, Kelly, Shanks, Davies, Cullen, Gregory, Groves, Adam
Apprentice Tony Gregory, 18, nets his first home goal with a fine shot. South African Roy Davies chases a loose ball and puts Dally Duncan's men further ahead. Sillett nets from the spot after a foul on Bentley. Chelsea show new heart and Dicks' solo effort is his first goal for the club.

37. H Preston — 0-1
Scorers: — / Finney 22p
Ref: G Oliver
Chelsea: Robertson, Sillett, Willemse, Dicks, Wicks, Casey, Parsons, McNichol, Bentley, Stubbs, Blunstone
Preston: Else, Cunningham, Walton, Docherty, Dunn, Wilson, Finney, Thompson T, Hatsell, Baxter, Campbell
Young keeper Fred Else defies Chelsea with fine saves. A shot from Jim Baxter is parried and caught by Willemse – the clearest of penalties, which Tom Finney nets. Frank Hill's men hang on, but the game is so dull the crowd seems more interested in a fire visible outside the ground!

38. H Luton — 0-0
Ref: F Coultas
Chelsea: Robertson, Harris, Willemse, Nicholas, Wicks, Casey, Lewis, Brabrook, Tindall, Bentley, Blunstone
Luton: Baynham, Dunne, Jones, Morton, Kelly, Shanks, Cullen, Pemberton, Gregory, Groves, Adam
Drake makes a number of changes, including the recall of veteran Harris. Chelsea record their eighth league game without a win; the defending champions are drifting embarrassingly close to the relegation zone. The mid-table Hatters have also had a winless Easter. This is a drab affair.

39. A Sheffield Utd — 1-2
Scorers: Tindall 42 / Howitt 15, Grainger 27
Ref: J Swain
Chelsea: Robertson, Harris, Willemse, Nicholas, Wicks, Casey, Lewis, Brabrook, Tindall, Bentley, Stubbs
Sheffield Utd: Burgin, Coldwell, Mason, Hoyland, Johnson, Iley, Ringstead, Hagan, Wilkinson, Howitt, Grainger
Both sides are desperate for points to avoid the drop. Sillett blocks a shot on the line but Howitt returns it into goal. Wicks stops Hagan's shot, but Grainger is on hand for the second. Tindall pulls one back, steering in a Lewis pass. The win is just temporary relief for boss Joe Mercer.

40. H Everton — 6-1
Scorers: Bentley 12, 57, 77, Stubbs 15, 71, [Lewis 88] / Harris 72
Ref: S Rogers
Chelsea: Robertson, Sillett, Willemse, Saunders, Wicks, Casey, Lewis, Brabrook, Bentley, Tindall, Stubbs
Everton: Harris, Moore, Tansey, Birch, Jones, Farrell, Harris B, Donovan, Harris J, Fielding, Eglington
Two points should be enough for safety and Cliff Britton's side look in poor shape. Scotland v England on TV keeps the fans away. They miss a fine Bentley hat-trick, featuring a long-range rocket, two by the marauding Stubbs and a dazzling run by Blunstone that sets up the final goal.

41. A Newcastle — 1-1
Scorers: Stubbs 1 / Milburn 89p
Ref: N Hough
Chelsea: Robertson, Sillett, Willemse, Saunders, Wicks, Casey, Lewis, Brabrook, Bentley, Tindall, Stubbs
Newcastle: Simpson, Batty, McMichael, Scoular, White, Casey T, Harris, Milburn, Keeble, Currie, Mitchell
Blunstone nips past Jimmy Scoular to cross for Stubbs' early strike. Tom Casey and Vic Keeble are 'passengers' after injury. Willemse clears off the line from Bill Curry but Chelsea let a point slip near the end when Saunders fouls Bobby Mitchell. Jackie Milburn slides in the penalty.

42. H Blackpool — 2-1
Scorers: Bentley 7, 25 / Durie 4
Ref: E Oxley
Chelsea: Robertson, Whittaker, Sillett, Mortimore, Wicks, Compton, Lewis, Brabrook, Bentley, Stubbs, Blunstone
Blackpool: Farm, Armfield, Wright, Kelly J, Snowdon, Kelly H, Harris, Taylor, Mudie, Durie, Perry
Irishman Dick Whittaker, John Mortimore (ex-Woking) and youngster John Compton all get debuts. Jackie Mudie feeds Dave Durie for a neat goal, but Bentley hits straight back from a Blunstone pull-back. Bentley soars high to head the second. A disappointing season ends in victory.

LEAGUE DIVISION 1 (CUP-TIES)   Manager: Ted Drake   SEASON 1955-56

FA Cup				Att	Pos		F-A	H-T	Scorers, Times, and Referees	1	2	3	4	5	6	7	8	9	10	11
3	A	HARTLEPOOLS	12	16,700 3McB		W	1-0	1-0	Moore 23 (og)	Robertson	Sillett	Willemse	Dicks	Wicks	Saunders	Parsons	McNichol	Bentley	Stubbs	Blunstone
	7/1								Ref: J Topliss	*Dyson*	*Cameron*	*Thompson*	*Newton*	*Moore*	*Stamper*	*Rayment*	*Lumley*	*Johnson*	*McGuigan*	*Luke*

Fred Westgarth's enthusiastic side ruffle the champs' feathers and it takes a freak goal to win the tie. Keeper Jack Dyson parries a cross which hits Watty Moore and rolls goalwards. In attempting to hit it clear, Moore helps it into the net. Robertson makes a wonderful last-minute save.

FA Cup				Att	Pos		F-A	H-T	Scorers, Times, and Referees	1	2	3	4	5	6	7	8	9	10	11
4	A	BURNLEY	13	44,897 5		D	1-1	0-1	Parsons 85	Robertson	Sillett	Willemse	Dicks	Wicks	Saunders	Parsons	McNichol	Bentley	Stubbs	Blunstone
	28/1								McKay 5	*McDonald*	*Rudman*	*Winton*	*Seith*	*Cummings*	*Adamson*	*Gray*	*McIlroy*	*McKay*	*Cheesebrough Pilkington*	*Cheesebrough Pilkington*
									Ref: J Pickles											

Alan Brown's side hit a post early after a melee and then go ahead through Peter McKay. Chelsea fight hard but their cup dream looks doomed until the dying minutes when Parsons pops up to force an unexpected replay. Elsewhere there are no cup shocks as the big guns ease through.

FA Cup				Att	Pos		F-A	H-T	Scorers, Times, and Referees	1	2	3	4	5	6	7	8	9	10	11
4R	H	BURNLEY	13	=6,661 5		D	1-1	0-0	Blunstone 55	Robertson	Sillett	Willemse	Dicks	Wicks	Saunders	Parsons	McNichol	Bentley	Stubbs	Blunstone
	1/2							aet	Pilkington 70	*McDonald*	*Cummings*	*Winton*	*Seith*	*Adamson*	*Miller*	*Gray*	*McIlroy*	*McKay*	*Cheesebrough Pilkington*	*Cheesebrough Pilkington*
									Ref: J Pickles											

Blunstone lobs keeper Colin McDonald after young Brian Miller slips on the icy pitch. Brian Pilkington races past a sluggish-looking Sillett to cross and after several efforts on goal by teammates, Pilkington pops up to nod the loose ball in himself. Peter McKay hits a post in extra-time.

FA Cup				Att	Pos		F-A	H-T	Scorers, Times, and Referees	1	2	3	4	5	6	7	8	9	10	11
4	N	BURNLEY	13	2x,921 5		D	2-2	1-1	Sillett 33p, Bentley 76	Robertson	Sillett	Willemse	Dicks	Wicks	Saunders	Parsons	Brabrook	Tindall	Bentley	Blunstone
2R	6/2	(at Birmingham)						aet	McKay 20, McIlroy 48	*McDonald*	*Cummings*	*Winton*	*Seith*	*Adamson*	*Miller*	*Gray*	*McIlroy*	*McKay*	*Cheesebrough Pilkington*	*Cheesebrough Pilkington*
									Ref: J Pickles											

Peter McKay is teed up by Billy Gray. Chelsea look ponderous in defence and at one point a limping Sillett has an angry exchange with the crowd. After Brabrook is floored, Sillett nets from the spot. Jimmy McIlroy shoots a superb goal before Bentley pounces on a slip to equalise.

FA Cup				Att	Pos		F-A	H-T	Scorers, Times, and Referees	1	2	3	4	5	6	7	8	9	10	11
4	N	BURNLEY	13	4x,757 5		D	0-0	0-0		Thomson	Sillett	Willemse	Nicholas	Wicks	Saunders	Parsons	McNichol	Bentley	Stubbs	Blunstone
3R	13/2	(at Arsenal)						aet	Ref: R Smith	*McDonald*	*Cummings*	*Winton*	*Seith*	*Adamson*	*Shannon*	*Newlands*	*McIlroy*	*McKay*	*Cheesebrough Pilkington*	*Cheesebrough Pilkington*

Here we go again. The FA is insisting the fifth round tie must go ahead this Saturday, but still no result is forthcoming tonight. Peter McKay goes closest, having a goal disallowed for offside. It's a heavy pitch and 22 weary players must now make their way to Tottenham in 48 hours.

FA Cup				Att	Pos		F-A	H-T	Scorers, Times, and Referees	1	2	3	4	5	6	7	8	9	10	11
4	N	BURNLEY	13	27,210 5		W	2-0	1-0	Tindall 36, Lewis 81	Thomson	Sillett	Willemse	Nicholas	Livingstone	Saunders	Lewis	McNichol	Bentley	Tindall	Blunstone
4R	15/2	(at Tottenham)							Ref: L Callaghan	*McDonald*	*Rudman*	*Winton*	*Seith*	*Cummings*	*Shannon*	*Gray*	*McIlroy*	*McKay*	*Cheesebrough Pilkington*	*Cheesebrough Pilkington*

The FA suggests an hour of extra time if needed tonight, but Drake won't agree to this. The fifth meeting in 18 days is finally settled after nine hours (equalling the FA Cup record). Scot Bill Livingstone (ex-Reading) debuts. Tindall and Lewis pounce on errors to send Chelsea through.

FA Cup				Att	Pos		F-A	H-T	Scorers, Times, and Referees	1	2	3	4	5	6	7	8	9	10	11
5	A	EVERTON	14	61,572 10		L	0-1	0-1	Farrell 14	Thomson	Sillett	Willemse	Nicholas	Wicks	Saunders	Lewis	McNichol	Bentley	Tindall	Blunstone
	18/2								Ref: R Mann	*Leyland*	*Moore*	*Tansey*	*Farrell*	*Jones*	*Lello*	*Harris B*	*Wainwright*	*Harris J*	*Fielding*	*Eglington*

Peter Farrell's superbly worked early goal on an icy pitch is decisive. Drake's weary men battle bravely but the manager's F.A. Cup dream dies. He says he is proud of how they fought in their fourth game in eight days. A victim of the fourth round marathon was Parsons, absent with flu.

League table

	P	W	D	L	F	A	W	D	L	F	A	Pts
				Home						Away		
1 Manchester U	42	18	3	0	51	20	7	7	7	32	31	60
2 Blackpool	42	13	4	4	56	27	7	9	9	30	35	49
3 Wolves	42	15	2	4	51	27	5	7	9	38	38	49
4 Manchester C	42	11	5	5	40	27	7	5	9	42	42	46
5 Arsenal	42	13	4	4	38	22	5	6	10	42	39	46
6 Birmingham	42	12	4	5	51	26	6	5	10	24	31	45
7 Burnley	42	11	3	7	37	20	5	7	9	27	34	44
8 Bolton	42	13	3	5	50	24	5	4	12	21	34	43
9 Sunderland	42	10	8	3	44	36	7	1	13	36	59	43
10 Luton	42	12	4	5	44	27	5	4	12	22	37	42
11 Newcastle	42	12	4	5	49	24	5	3	13	36	46	41
12 Portsmouth	42	9	8	4	46	38	7	1	13	32	47	41
13 West Brom	42	13	3	5	37	25	5	2	14	21	45	41
14 Charlton	42	12	3	6	47	26	4	4	13	28	55	40
15 Everton	42	11	5	5	37	29	4	5	12	18	40	40
16 CHELSEA	42	10	4	7	32	26	4	7	10	32	51	39
17 Cardiff	42	11	4	6	36	32	4	5	12	19	37	39
18 Tottenham	42	9	9	8	37	33	6	3	12	24	38	37
19 Preston	42	6	5	10	32	36	8	3	11	41	36	36
20 Aston Villa	42	9	6	6	32	29	2	7	12	20	40	35
21 Huddersfield	42	9	4	8	32	30	5	3	13	22	53	35
22 Sheffield Utd	42	8	6	7	31	35	4	3	14	32	42	33
	924	248	95	119	910	619	119	95	248	619	910	924

Odds & ends

Double wins: (1) Charlton.

Double losses: (5) Birmingham, Bolton, Man U, Sunderland, Wolves.

Won from behind: (4) Villa (a), Blackpool (h), Preston (a), Man C (h).

Lost from in front: (5) Birmingham (h), Manchester U (h), Sunderland (a), Wolves (h&a).

High spots: Smashing six past Everton to ensure safety.

Capturing the signature of 15-year-old Jimmy Greaves.

Low spots: Inconsistency and poor form post-Christmas.

Going out of the FA Cup after being forced to play six ties in 21 days.

Plummeting from first to 21st, between May and September 1955.

Tossing away a 3-0 lead at Portsmouth.

'Doubled' by Wolves, despite leading in both games.

Note: The nine-hour Cup-tie with Burnley equalled the all-time record.

Appearances and Goals

Player	App Lge	App FAC	Goals Lge	Goals FAC	Goals Tot
Armstrong, Ken	24				
Bellett, Walter	2				
Bentley, Roy	38	7	14	1	15
Blunstone, Frank	41	7	6	1	7
Brabrook, Peter	18	1	3		3
Casey, Len	7				
Compton, John	1				
Dicks, Alan	4	4	1		1
Harris, John	3				
Kitchener, Ray	1				
Lewis, Jim	9	2	2	1	3
Livingstone, Bill	1				
McNichol, Johnny	24	6	2		2
Mortimore, John	1				
Nicholas, Brian	10	3			
O'Connell, Seamus	6		4		4
Parsons, Eric	33	5	7	1	8
Robertson, Bill	34	4			
Saunders, Derek	37	7			
Sillett, Peter	41	7	2	1	3
Smith, Bobby	7		4		4
Stubbs, Les	17	4	10		10
Thomson, Charlie	8	3			
Tindall, Ron	15	3	7	1	8
Whittaker, Dick	1				
Wicks, Stan	42	6			
Willemse, Stan	38	7	2	1	3
(own-goals)					
27 players used	462	77	64	7	67

Hat-tricks: (2) Blunstone (v Portsmouth, a), Bentley (v Everton, h).

Opposing hat-tricks: (2) Lofthouse (Bolton), Brian Pilkington (Burnley).

Ever-presents: (1) Stan Wicks.

Leading scorer: (15) Roy Bentley.

The Daily Express explains how the championship was won,
with Chelsea still having one game to play (April 1955)